I0012471

BUILDING APIS WITH NODE.JS

A Guide to RESTful APIs

THOMPSON CARTER

TABLE OF CONTENTS

Introduction

In the rapidly evolving digital landscape, Application Programming Interfaces (APIs) are the backbone of modern web services. APIs enable different software applications to communicate with one another, allowing for seamless integration and the sharing of data. Whether you are building a web application, mobile app, or even a microservice architecture, APIs have become essential tools in connecting systems and creating robust, scalable solutions.

At the forefront of API development today is **Node.js**, a powerful, JavaScript-based runtime environment that has become a popular choice for building fast, efficient, and scalable APIs. With its non-blocking, event-driven architecture, Node.js is well-suited to handle concurrent requests, making it ideal for building APIs that must serve a large number of users simultaneously.

This book, **Building APIs with Node.js: A Guide to RESTful APIs**, is designed to help you become proficient in creating high-performance, scalable APIs using Node.js. Whether you are a beginner or have some experience with web development, this book will guide you step-by-step through the entire process of building robust, production-ready APIs. With a practical, hands-on approach, you'll gain a deep understanding of the fundamental concepts, tools, and techniques required to build, test, secure, and deploy APIs using Node.js.

Why Node.js for API Development?

Node.js has become one of the most popular platforms for building APIs for several reasons:

1. **JavaScript Everywhere**: Node.js allows developers to use JavaScript on both the server and the client side. This makes it easier to manage your codebase, as you don't need to switch between different programming languages. As JavaScript is the most widely used language for web development, Node.js benefits from its large, active community and rich ecosystem of libraries and tools.

2. **Non-Blocking, Event-Driven Architecture**: Node.js uses a non-blocking, event-driven model, which makes it highly efficient for handling a large number of simultaneous connections with minimal overhead. This is particularly important when building APIs that need to handle high levels of traffic.

3. **Asynchronous I/O**: Node.js handles I/O operations asynchronously, meaning that the server doesn't have to wait for tasks like file reading, database queries, or HTTP requests to complete before moving on to the next task.

This improves the performance and scalability of your API, especially under load.

4. **Large Ecosystem**: Node.js has a vast collection of libraries and frameworks, such as **Express.js**, which simplify the process of building APIs. These frameworks provide out-of-the-box features for routing, middleware handling, and more, allowing you to focus on writing application-specific logic.

5. **Scalability**: Node.js is ideal for building APIs that need to scale horizontally (across multiple servers) due to its event-driven, non-blocking nature. This makes it well-suited for modern, microservice-based architectures where APIs are often used in tandem with other services.

What This Book Will Cover

In this book, we will take a hands-on, practical approach to building APIs with Node.js. We will begin with the basics, ensuring that you have a solid understanding of what APIs are, how they work, and why they are so crucial for modern web development. We will then dive into the tools and technologies you will use to build your API, with a particular focus on **Express.js**, a minimal, flexible Node.js web application framework that simplifies the process of building APIs.

Here's a breakdown of what you will learn throughout the chapters:

Part 1: Introduction to Node.js and APIs

We begin with an overview of APIs and introduce you to Node.js, explaining its role in API development. You will learn about **RESTful APIs**, the most common type of API used today, and gain an understanding of how Node.js fits into this landscape. We will also cover the setup process for your development environment, including installing Node.js, configuring your editor, and preparing tools like **Postman** for testing your API endpoints.

Part 2: Building Core API Features

Once your environment is set up, we will dive into building your first API with **Express.js**. You'll learn how to create routes, handle HTTP requests, and understand the difference between various HTTP methods such as GET, POST, PUT, and DELETE. By the end of this part, you'll have a working API that can handle basic CRUD operations (Create, Read, Update, Delete).

Part 3: Enhancing Your API

As your API becomes more feature-rich, you will encounter additional requirements such as **data validation**, **error handling**, and **working with external services**. You will also learn how to connect your API to a database—both SQL and NoSQL—to store and manage data. By the end of this part, you'll know how to create a dynamic API capable of handling complex operations and real-world use cases.

Part 4: Authentication and Security

Security is one of the most critical aspects of API development. In this part, we'll cover **authentication** methods such as **JWT (JSON Web Tokens)** and **OAuth** to ensure that only authorized users can access your API. You'll also learn about best practices for securing your API, such as implementing HTTPS, role-based access control, and protecting sensitive data.

Part 5: Advanced API Features

In this section, we will explore more advanced topics such as **file uploads**, **integrating with third-party APIs**, and **versioning** your API to ensure backward compatibility. We'll also look into performance optimization techniques like **rate-limiting** and **caching** to ensure that your API can handle large traffic volumes without degrading in performance.

Part 6: Testing, Documentation, and Deployment

The final part of the book focuses on preparing your API for production. You will learn how to test your API using tools like **Mocha** and **Chai**, ensuring that your routes and authentication mechanisms work as expected. We'll then walk through how to document your API with **Swagger**, making it easier for other developers to understand and integrate with your service. Finally, we'll cover deployment to popular cloud platforms like **Heroku** and **AWS**, ensuring that your API is production-ready and scalable.

Why This Book is Different

While many tutorials on Node.js and API development are filled with jargon and abstract concepts, this book is designed to be as **practical** and **accessible** as possible. We focus on real-world examples and ensure that every chapter includes hands-on coding exercises, so you can apply what you learn immediately. By the end of the book, you will have the skills to build production-ready, scalable APIs using Node.js.

Additionally, we make a conscious effort to avoid technical jargon where possible, ensuring that even if you are new to backend development, you can follow along and understand the material.

Who This Book is For

This book is ideal for:

- **Beginner web developers** who are familiar with JavaScript and want to dive into backend development with Node.js.
- **Front-end developers** looking to expand their skillset by learning how to build APIs.
- **Intermediate developers** who want to deepen their understanding of Node.js and API design.
- **Students** or **hobbyists** who are passionate about building real-world applications and APIs.

By following this guide, you will not only learn how to build APIs but also gain the necessary skills to optimize, secure, and deploy them in real-world environments. Whether you're looking to create a small app or work on large-scale enterprise projects, this book will provide you with the knowledge and hands-on experience to succeed.

So, let's dive into the world of API development with Node.js and start building powerful, scalable, and secure APIs that can drive your next great project!

Chapter 1: Introduction to APIs and Node.js

What Are APIs?

APIs (Application Programming Interfaces) are an essential component in modern software development, allowing different applications or services to communicate and share data. In simple terms, an API defines a set of rules that govern how software components interact with each other. APIs allow developers to access specific features or data from an external service or system in a standardized way.

APIs are everywhere. Whether you're checking the weather, logging into a website, or interacting with social media platforms, APIs are the unseen engines powering these interactions. For instance, when you use an app on your phone to check the weather, it may be pulling data from a weather service API to provide the latest forecast. The same goes for mobile apps and websites that pull data from databases, display dynamic content, or integrate external services.

Key concepts related to APIs:

- **End Points**: An endpoint is a URL where an API can access the resources it needs.

- **Methods**: APIs work using standard HTTP methods like GET, POST, PUT, and DELETE, each designed for a specific action (retrieving data, submitting data, updating, or deleting data).
- **JSON (JavaScript Object Notation)**: Most modern APIs communicate using JSON, a lightweight format for transmitting data that's easy for both humans and machines to read and write.

APIs are essential because they allow different software applications to connect, enabling developers to leverage existing functionality and services without having to build everything from scratch. Whether it's accessing payment gateways like PayPal, social media integrations, or payment processing, APIs are the bridge that connects various software systems.

Introduction to Node.js and Its Role in API Development

Node.js is an open-source, cross-platform runtime environment that allows developers to execute JavaScript code on the server side. Unlike traditional JavaScript, which is mainly used for client-side scripting in web browsers, Node.js allows JavaScript to be run on the server, making it a powerful tool for building web applications, including APIs.

Node.js is built on the **V8 JavaScript engine**, the same engine used by Google Chrome, and is known for its speed, scalability, and efficiency. One of the key features of Node.js is its **non-blocking, event-driven architecture**, which makes it particularly well-suited for I/O-heavy operations, such as reading files, making network requests, or accessing databases. This makes Node.js a popular choice for building scalable, high-performance applications like APIs.

In the context of API development, Node.js offers several benefits:

- **Asynchronous and Event-Driven**: Node.js can handle multiple requests simultaneously without blocking other processes. This makes it ideal for building APIs that need to handle many concurrent requests efficiently.

- **Fast and Lightweight**: Node.js is extremely fast due to its event-driven nature and use of the V8 engine, which compiles JavaScript to machine code for optimal performance.

- **Single Language for Both Client and Server**: Node.js allows developers to use JavaScript on both the front-end and back-end, simplifying the development process and reducing the learning curve for developers who are already familiar with JavaScript.

- **Rich Ecosystem**: With npm (Node Package Manager), Node.js developers have access to a vast library of packages and modules, which can greatly speed up development time when building APIs.

Benefits of Using Node.js for Building APIs

1. **Performance**: Due to its event-driven, non-blocking architecture, Node.js can handle thousands of concurrent connections with minimal overhead, making it ideal for building high-performance APIs. This is especially important for real-time applications like chat apps, social media platforms, or any API that needs to handle high traffic.

2. **Scalability**: Node.js is designed to be scalable. Whether you're building a small RESTful API for a personal project or a large-scale API for an enterprise-level application, Node.js allows for easy scaling. It supports horizontal scaling (running multiple instances of your application across different servers) and vertical scaling (adding more resources to the existing server).

3. **Real-Time Data**: Node.js is particularly well-suited for real-time applications, such as messaging platforms, collaboration tools, or any API that requires instant communication. Its ability to handle multiple simultaneous

connections without compromising performance makes it a great choice for these types of applications.

4. **Ease of Use**: Node.js is relatively easy to learn, especially for developers who are already familiar with JavaScript. With a single language for both front-end and back-end, developers can work seamlessly across the entire stack, reducing development time and complexity.

5. **Extensive Libraries and Frameworks**: Node.js has a rich ecosystem of libraries and frameworks, making it easy to build APIs quickly and efficiently. Popular frameworks like **Express.js** simplify the process of setting up and managing routes, middleware, and error handling in your API.

6. **Community and Support**: Node.js has a vibrant community of developers who contribute to a wide variety of open-source libraries and tools. Whether you're building a simple RESTful API or a complex, enterprise-level application, you'll find plenty of resources, tutorials, and community support to help you.

Why Choose Node.js for Your API Development?

When compared to other programming languages and frameworks, Node.js stands out in several areas, particularly in terms of performance, scalability, and ease of use. Its non-blocking, event-driven nature is highly effective for building APIs that need to handle large volumes of concurrent requests efficiently.

Moreover, with a single language (JavaScript) used both on the client and server-side, Node.js offers a more streamlined development process, especially for full-stack developers. Using Node.js also allows for quicker iteration and deployment of APIs, which is crucial in today's fast-paced development cycles.

In this chapter, we've covered the fundamentals of APIs, their importance in modern web development, and the role of Node.js in API creation. Whether you're building a simple API or a complex, real-time web service, Node.js offers the tools and performance needed to create scalable, high-performance APIs. In the next chapters, we will dive deeper into how to set up and develop RESTful APIs using Node.js, exploring core concepts like routing, data handling, security, and more. By the end of this book, you'll have the knowledge and skills to build powerful and efficient APIs using Node.js.

Chapter 2: Understanding RESTful APIs

What is REST (Representational State Transfer)?

REST, or **Representational State Transfer**, is an architectural style used for designing networked applications. It is based on a stateless, client-server communication model where requests from clients are made to a server, and the server responds with the requested resources or data. RESTful APIs are designed to be lightweight, fast, and easy to scale, making them ideal for web services that need to interact with different applications or platforms.

The term **REST** was first introduced by **Roy Fielding** in his doctoral dissertation in 2000, and it has since become one of the most widely used architectural styles for building web services. REST is not a protocol or a standard but rather a set of guidelines or principles that promote a more scalable and maintainable architecture.

The main characteristic of a RESTful API is that it uses **HTTP** methods (GET, POST, PUT, DELETE, etc.) to perform actions on resources. Resources in REST are represented as **URLs (Uniform Resource Locators)**, which point to entities or objects on the server, such as user profiles, blog posts, or product data. When a client makes an HTTP request to the API, it retrieves or manipulates these resources.

Principles of REST Architecture

REST follows a set of principles that help developers build scalable, maintainable, and loosely-coupled web services. These principles are:

1. **Statelessness**:
   - In a RESTful system, each request from the client to the server must contain all the information needed to understand and process the request. The server does not store any client context between requests. This statelessness means that each request is independent and contains all the necessary data, which makes the system more scalable and fault-tolerant.
   - Example: When you log in to a website, the server does not store your login credentials or session information for subsequent requests. Instead, your client (e.g., browser or app) stores this information in a cookie or token and sends it with each request.

2. **Client-Server Architecture**:
   - RESTful APIs follow a **client-server** architecture, where the client and server are separate entities that communicate via HTTP requests. The client (usually the front-end application) is responsible for

the user interface and interactions, while the server (often the back-end) handles business logic, data storage, and API responses.

o This separation allows each part to be developed, updated, and scaled independently. Clients and servers can evolve separately without affecting each other, as long as the agreed-upon API contract (the set of available endpoints and their behavior) is maintained.

3. **Uniform Interface**:

o A key principle of REST is the use of a **uniform interface**, which simplifies the architecture by standardizing how clients interact with the server. This includes using standard HTTP methods (GET, POST, PUT, DELETE) and defining clear, logical resource names (URLs) for accessing data.

o Example: A RESTful API might use the following endpoints:

  - GET /users – to get a list of users
  - POST /users – to create a new user
  - GET /users/{id} – to get a specific user by ID
  - PUT /users/{id} – to update a specific user by ID
  - DELETE /users/{id} – to delete a specific user by ID

4. **Stateless Communications**:

   o As mentioned earlier, each request to a RESTful API is stateless, meaning the server does not maintain any session information. Each request must contain all necessary information for the server to fulfill the request. This makes RESTful APIs scalable and easier to cache, as no server-side memory is needed.

5. **Cacheability**:

   o In RESTful systems, responses should be explicitly marked as **cacheable** or **non-cacheable** to improve performance. When data is cacheable, it can be stored by the client (or intermediate caches) to avoid repetitive calls to the server.

   o Example: A weather API might mark weather data as cacheable for a short time period (e.g., 10 minutes), allowing clients to store the response and avoid fetching the same data repeatedly.

6. **Layered System**:

   o A RESTful architecture may be composed of multiple layers, such as caching layers, load balancers, and security layers, between the client and the server. These layers interact with each other but are not visible to the client. Each layer should be independent and offer specific functionality.

- o Example: A load balancer might distribute client requests to different servers based on traffic, while the client remains unaware of this process.

7. **Code on Demand (Optional)**:
   - o In some cases, a RESTful API may allow the server to send executable code to the client, such as JavaScript or other scripts, which can be executed in the client's environment. This is the optional **code-on-demand** feature, which enhances the functionality of the client.
   - o Example: When visiting a website, the server may send a script to your browser to update a page's content dynamically (e.g., with JavaScript).

Real-World Examples of RESTful APIs

Many popular platforms and services use RESTful APIs to provide developers with easy-to-use interfaces for integrating their data and functionality into other applications. Let's take a look at a few real-world examples of RESTful APIs:

1. **GitHub API**:
   - o GitHub provides a RESTful API that allows developers to interact programmatically with repositories, pull requests, issues, users, and other

GitHub features. Using GitHub's API, you can create new repositories, list user repositories, fetch pull requests, and much more. The GitHub API is widely used by developers for automating tasks, integrating with other tools, and accessing repository data.

Example request:

- o GET /users/{username}/repos – Fetch a list of repositories for a specific user.

2. **Twitter API**:

- o Twitter's RESTful API enables developers to access and interact with Twitter data programmatically. With this API, developers can send tweets, read timelines, search for tweets, follow users, and more. Twitter's API provides essential features for social media management tools, analytics platforms, and other applications.

Example request:

- o GET /statuses/user_timeline – Fetch a list of recent tweets from a user.

3. **Spotify API**:

- o Spotify provides a RESTful API that allows developers to access its music catalog, manage playlists, retrieve album information, and more. The Spotify API is used by various music-related applications and services to integrate Spotify's music data and features.

Example request:

o GET /v1/me/top/artists – Retrieve the current user's top artists.

4. **OpenWeatherMap API**:
   o OpenWeatherMap offers a RESTful API for retrieving weather data. Developers can access real-time weather information, forecasts, historical data, and more for any location in the world. This API is commonly used in weather apps, websites, and IoT devices.

Example request:

o GET   /data/2.5/weather?q={city}&appid={API_KEY} – Fetch current weather for a specific city.

Understanding RESTful APIs is crucial for building modern web services and applications. By following the principles of REST, developers can create APIs that are efficient, scalable, and easy to use. RESTful APIs have become the standard for web development because of their simplicity, flexibility, and power. In the next chapters, we will explore how to use Node.js to build powerful RESTful APIs from scratch, learning how to handle routing, manage data, and implement security and performance optimizations.

Chapter 3: Setting Up Your Development Environment

In this chapter, we'll guide you through setting up a development environment that allows you to build, test, and deploy RESTful APIs using Node.js. A proper setup will ensure that you can quickly start writing code, troubleshoot issues efficiently, and test your APIs in a streamlined manner. We'll cover the installation of Node.js, the use of npm (Node Package Manager), setting up a code editor (VS Code), and how to use Postman for API testing.

---

1. Installing Node.js and npm

Node.js is a JavaScript runtime built on Chrome's V8 JavaScript engine, which is essential for running JavaScript code outside of a browser. When building RESTful APIs, Node.js provides the server-side environment, allowing you to execute your API logic.

npm (Node Package Manager) comes bundled with Node.js and is used to manage JavaScript packages or libraries that you can use to simplify API development. With npm, you can install various libraries, frameworks, and tools that will aid in building APIs, such as Express.js, a lightweight web framework for Node.js.

Steps to Install Node.js and npm:

1. **Download Node.js:**
   - o Visit the official Node.js website: https://nodejs.org.
   - o Download the LTS (Long Term Support) version, which is the most stable and recommended for most developers.

2. **Install Node.js:**
   - o Once the installer is downloaded, run it and follow the installation instructions for your operating system.
   - o The installation process will automatically install both Node.js and npm.

3. **Verify Installation:**
   - o Open your terminal (Command Prompt on Windows, Terminal on macOS/Linux).
   - o Type the following command to verify Node.js installation:

   bash

   node -v

   This should display the version of Node.js installed.

   - o To verify npm installation, type:

   bash

```
npm -v
```

This will display the version of npm.

---

2. Setting Up a Code Editor (e.g., VS Code)

A **code editor** is an essential tool for writing and editing your code. **Visual Studio Code (VS Code)** is one of the most popular code editors, especially for JavaScript and Node.js development. It's lightweight, feature-rich, and comes with powerful extensions for API development.

Steps to Install VS Code:

1. **Download VS Code:**
   o Go to the official VS Code website: https://code.visualstudio.com.
   o Download the installer appropriate for your operating system.

2. **Install VS Code:**
   o Run the installer and follow the on-screen instructions.

3. **Add Node.js Extensions:**
   o Once installed, open VS Code.

- o Go to the **Extensions** view by clicking on the Extensions icon on the sidebar (or pressing Ctrl+Shift+X).
- o In the search bar, type **Node.js** to install extensions such as:
  - **Node.js Extension Pack** – A collection of tools for Node.js development.
  - **ESLint** – A popular linting tool to keep your JavaScript code clean and error-free.
  - **Prettier** – A code formatter for consistent formatting.

4. **Customizing VS Code:**
   - o You can customize VS Code's theme, font, and layout to suit your personal preferences, making your development environment more efficient and comfortable.

---

3. Introduction to Postman for API Testing

Postman is a powerful tool for testing and interacting with APIs. It allows you to send HTTP requests to your API endpoints and inspect the responses, helping you validate that your API is functioning correctly. Postman simplifies the process of making requests and handling responses with a user-friendly interface, which is crucial for testing and debugging your APIs.

Steps to Install and Use Postman:

1. **Download Postman:**
   - Visit the official Postman website: https://www.postman.com/downloads.
   - Download the version of Postman appropriate for your operating system.

2. **Install Postman:**
   - Run the installer and follow the on-screen instructions.

3. **Using Postman for API Testing:**
   - Once installed, open Postman. You'll see the main workspace where you can create new requests.
   - Click on the **New** button, then select **Request** to create a new API request.
   - In the **Request** tab:
     - Choose the **HTTP method** (GET, POST, PUT, DELETE) based on the type of request you want to make.
     - Enter the **URL** of the endpoint you wish to test (e.g., http://localhost:3000/api/users).
     - If necessary, add headers, parameters, or a request body (for POST and PUT requests).
   - Click **Send** to send the request to your API.
   - The **Response** section will show the status code, response body, headers, and other information.

- You can check if your API returns the correct data, handles errors properly, and responds with the appropriate HTTP status codes (e.g., 200 for success, 404 for not found).

4. **Using Collections and Environments:**
   - Postman allows you to group related requests into **Collections**, making it easier to organize and manage your API tests.
   - You can also create **Environments** with variables (e.g., base URLs, API keys) that you can switch between easily, making testing across different environments (local, staging, production) seamless.

By setting up your development environment with Node.js, npm, VS Code, and Postman, you're well-equipped to start building and testing your RESTful APIs. Node.js offers a robust and scalable foundation for API development, and tools like Postman will simplify your testing process. In the next chapters, we'll dive into creating your first API, handling routing, and interacting with databases, which will allow you to create a fully functional API using Node.js.

Chapter 4: First Steps with Express.js

Express.js is one of the most popular frameworks for building RESTful APIs with Node.js. Its simplicity, flexibility, and robustness make it a go-to choice for developers who want to create server-side applications efficiently. In this chapter, we'll introduce Express.js, set up your first Express server, and explain key concepts such as routes and middleware, which are foundational to building APIs.

What is Express.js and Why Use It?

Express.js is a lightweight, fast, and flexible web application framework for Node.js. It provides a robust set of features for building web and mobile applications, with a focus on simplicity and minimalism.

Key Features of Express.js

1. **Lightweight Framework**: Express.js is unopinionated, meaning it provides core functionality while allowing you to structure your application as you see fit.
2. **Middleware Support**: Middleware functions enable you to process HTTP requests and responses seamlessly, adding powerful functionality like authentication, logging, and validation.

3. **Routing System**: Express simplifies routing, allowing you to define API endpoints with ease and handle HTTP methods like GET, POST, PUT, and DELETE.

4. **Integration with Databases**: Express works well with databases like MongoDB, MySQL, and PostgreSQL, making it a versatile choice for full-stack applications.

5. **Rich Ecosystem**: With an extensive library of npm packages, Express.js lets you quickly integrate additional functionality, such as file uploads, session management, and templating engines.

Why Use Express.js for API Development?

- **Ease of Use**: Express.js abstracts many of the complexities of Node.js, making API development faster and simpler.
- **Scalability**: Its modular design allows you to build small or large-scale applications with ease.
- **Community Support**: Express.js has a vibrant developer community, providing plenty of resources, tutorials, and plugins to enhance your projects.

Setting Up Your First Express Server

Now that you understand what Express.js is, let's set up a basic server.

1. **Initialize a Node.js Project**:
   - Create a new directory for your project and navigate to it in your terminal.

   bash

   ```
   mkdir express-api
   cd express-api
   ```

   - Initialize a Node.js project:

   bash

   ```
   npm init -y
   ```
   This will create a package.json file with default settings.

2. **Install Express.js**:
   - Install Express.js as a dependency:

   bash

   ```
   npm install express
   ```

---

1. **Create an Entry File**:

o Create a file named server.js or index.js in your project directory. This will be the entry point for your application.

2. **Set Up a Basic Express Server**: Add the following code to server.js:

javascript

```javascript
const express = require('express'); // Import Express
const app = express();          // Create an instance of Express

// Define a basic route
app.get('/', (req, res) => {
    res.send('Welcome to your first Express server!');
});

// Start the server
const PORT = 3000;
app.listen(PORT, () => {
    console.log(`Server is running on http://localhost:${PORT}`);
});
```

3. **Run the Server**:

o Start the server using Node.js:

bash

```bash
node server.js
```

o Open your browser and navigate to http://localhost:3000. You should see the message: **"Welcome to your first Express server!"**

Understanding Routes in Express

Routes in Express define how the server responds to specific HTTP requests. Each route is associated with an HTTP method (e.g., GET, POST, PUT, DELETE) and a URL path.

Defining Routes

Here's an example of defining routes for different HTTP methods:

javascript

```javascript
app.get('/users', (req, res) => {
    res.send('GET request to fetch all users');
});

app.post('/users', (req, res) => {
    res.send('POST request to create a new user');
});

app.put('/users/:id', (req, res) => {
    res.send(`PUT request to update user with ID ${req.params.id}`);
});

app.delete('/users/:id', (req, res) => {
    res.send(`DELETE request to delete user with ID ${req.params.id}`);
```

});

- **Path Parameters**: Use :id to define a dynamic segment in the URL path, which can be accessed via req.params.id.
- **Query Parameters**: Access query parameters (e.g., /users?sort=asc) via req.query.

Understanding Middleware

Middleware functions in Express.js are functions that execute during the lifecycle of a request to the server. Middleware can:

- Execute code.
- Modify the request and response objects.
- End the request-response cycle.
- Call the next middleware function in the stack.

Types of Middleware

1. **Built-in Middleware**:
    - **express.json()**: Parses incoming JSON payloads.
    - **express.urlencoded()**: Parses URL-encoded payloads.
2. **Third-Party Middleware**:
    - Middleware like cors or morgan can be installed to handle specific tasks.
3. **Custom Middleware**:

o You can write your own middleware to handle tasks like logging, authentication, or validation.

Using Middleware

Here's an example of middleware in action:

javascript

```
// Middleware function to log request details
app.use((req, res, next) => {
    console.log(`${req.method} request to ${req.url}`);
    next(); // Pass control to the next middleware or route
});

// Route handler
app.get('/', (req, res) => {
    res.send('Hello, Middleware!');
});
```

In this chapter, you learned about Express.js and its role in simplifying Node.js development. You set up your first Express server, created basic routes to handle HTTP requests, and explored middleware to enhance functionality. These building blocks are the foundation for developing scalable and maintainable APIs. In the next chapters, we'll dive deeper into handling requests, working with JSON data, and integrating databases to build more dynamic and robust RESTful APIs.

Chapter 5: Creating Routes and Handling Requests

In this chapter, we will focus on building the core structure of your RESTful API using Express.js by understanding how to define routes and handle HTTP requests effectively. HTTP methods such as GET, POST, PUT, and DELETE are integral to interacting with your API, and Express.js provides an intuitive way to handle them.

We will also explore how to process query parameters, request bodies, and URL parameters, all of which are common in most API interactions.

Introduction to HTTP Methods

HTTP methods (also known as HTTP verbs) define the action to be performed on a particular resource when a request is made. In a RESTful API, these methods correspond to CRUD (Create, Read, Update, Delete) operations, and they are key to defining the functionality of your API.

1. GET

- **Purpose**: Retrieves data from the server (Read operation).
- **Use Case**: When you want to fetch a list of items or a specific item.

- **Example**: Fetching all users or a specific user by ID.

2. POST

- **Purpose**: Sends data to the server to create a new resource (Create operation).
- **Use Case**: When you need to add a new resource to the database.
- **Example**: Creating a new user in the system.

3. PUT

- **Purpose**: Updates an existing resource on the server (Update operation).
- **Use Case**: When you need to modify an existing resource by sending the updated data.
- **Example**: Updating a user's profile information.

4. DELETE

- **Purpose**: Removes a resource from the server (Delete operation).
- **Use Case**: When you need to delete a resource.
- **Example**: Deleting a user from the database.

These HTTP methods are the foundation of building a RESTful API, and Express makes it easy to map them to specific routes in your application.

Defining API Routes in Express

Routes in Express are the paths that define the structure of your API endpoints. Each route corresponds to a specific HTTP method (GET, POST, PUT, DELETE) and a path that clients use to interact with your API.

Basic Route Setup

In Express, you define routes using the HTTP method-specific functions like .get(), .post(), .put(), and .delete(). These functions take two arguments:

1. **Path**: The URL path that identifies the endpoint.
2. **Callback function**: The function that handles the incoming request and sends back a response.

Here's an example of defining routes for each HTTP method:

javascript

```javascript
const express = require('express');
const app = express();

// GET Route: Fetch all users
```

```javascript
app.get('/users', (req, res) => {
    res.json({ message: 'List of all users' });
});


// POST Route: Create a new user
app.post('/users', (req, res) => {
    const user = req.body;  // Data sent in the request body
    res.status(201).json({ message: 'User created', user });
});


// PUT Route: Update an existing user by ID
app.put('/users/:id', (req, res) => {
    const { id } = req.params; // Path parameter (user ID)
    const updatedUser = req.body;  // Data sent in the request body
    res.json({ message: `User ${id} updated`, updatedUser });
});


// DELETE Route: Delete a user by ID
app.delete('/users/:id', (req, res) => {
    const { id } = req.params;  // Path parameter (user ID)
    res.json({ message: `User ${id} deleted` });
});


// Start the server
const PORT = 3000;
app.listen(PORT, () => {
    console.log(`Server is running on http://localhost:${PORT}`);
});
```

- **GET Route**: Fetches data without modifying anything. In this case, it returns a list of users.
- **POST Route**: Accepts data to create a new user.
- **PUT Route**: Takes an ID (via req.params) and the updated data (via req.body) to update a user.
- **DELETE Route**: Takes an ID (via req.params) and deletes the specified user.

Handling Query Parameters, Request Bodies, and URL Parameters

In many APIs, data is passed to the server via query parameters, request bodies, or URL parameters. Each type of data plays a different role in the request, and understanding how to handle them is crucial.

1. Query Parameters

Query parameters are used to filter, sort, or paginate data. They are passed in the URL after the ? symbol.

Example URL with Query Parameters:

bash

http://localhost:3000/users?name=John&age=30

In the above URL:

- name=John and age=30 are query parameters.

To access query parameters in Express, use req.query:

javascript

```
app.get('/users', (req, res) => {
    const { name, age } = req.query; // Extract query parameters
    res.json({ message: `Users filtered by name: ${name}, age: ${age}` });
});
```

2. URL Parameters

URL parameters (also known as route parameters) are part of the URL itself and are often used to identify specific resources. These are defined by placing a colon (:) in the route path.

Example URL with URL Parameters:

bash

```
http://localhost:3000/users/123
```

Here, 123 is the user ID. In Express, you can access URL parameters using req.params.

javascript

```
app.get('/users/:id', (req, res) => {
    const { id } = req.params;  // Access the user ID from the URL
    res.json({ message: `Fetching user with ID: ${id}` });
});
```

3. Request Body

When sending data to create or update a resource (typically in POST or PUT requests), the data is sent in the request body, often in JSON format. To handle this, you need to parse the body data before accessing it.

To enable parsing of JSON request bodies, use Express's built-in middleware express.json().

Example POST request with a request body:

json

```
{
    "name": "John Doe",
    "email": "john.doe@example.com"
}
```

To access the request body in Express:

javascript

```
app.use(express.json());  // Middleware to parse JSON body

app.post('/users', (req, res) => {
    const { name, email } = req.body;  // Access the data in the request body
    res.status(201).json({ message: 'User created', name, email });
});
```

In this chapter, you learned how to define and handle API routes using Express.js. We explored the core HTTP methods—GET, POST, PUT, and DELETE—and how they correspond to CRUD operations. You also learned how to work with query parameters, URL parameters, and request bodies, which are fundamental for building flexible and dynamic APIs.

With this knowledge, you are well-equipped to create RESTful routes for any application. In the next chapter, we'll dive deeper into handling errors, validating data, and managing responses, taking your API to the next level.

Chapter 6: Setting Up a Simple API

In this chapter, we'll walk through the steps of setting up a basic "Hello World" API using Node.js and Express. You'll learn how to handle GET requests and send responses, as well as how to structure your API routes for better organization and scalability.

By the end of this chapter, you'll have a simple API up and running, and you will understand the core concepts behind building RESTful APIs.

---

1. Building a Simple "Hello World" API

A "Hello World" API is the simplest form of an API, typically used to test that everything is working correctly. It responds to an HTTP request with a basic message, "Hello, World!"

Let's start by creating a minimal Node.js application and setting up an Express server.

Step-by-Step Guide

1. **Install Node.js**: If you haven't already, ensure that Node.js is installed on your computer. You can download it from nodejs.org.

2. **Create Your Project Folder**: In your terminal, navigate to the directory where you want to create your project and create a new folder for the API.

bash

```
mkdir hello-world-api
cd hello-world-api
```

3. **Initialize the Node.js Project**: Run the following command to initialize your Node.js project. This will create a package.json file that contains information about your project and its dependencies.

bash

```
npm init -y
```

4. **Install Express**: Express.js is a web framework for Node.js that makes it easier to build APIs. Install it using npm:

bash

```
npm install express
```

5. **Create the API Server**: Create an index.js file in your project folder and open it in your preferred code editor (e.g., Visual Studio Code).

javascript

```javascript
const express = require('express');
const app = express();

// Define a GET route for the root path
app.get('/', (req, res) => {
    res.send('Hello, World!');
});

// Start the server
const PORT = 3000;
app.listen(PORT, () => {
    console.log(`Server running at http://localhost:${PORT}`);
});
```

Here's what's happening:

- We first import the express module and create an instance of it.
- The app.get() method is used to define a route that listens for GET requests on the root path (/). When a request is made to this endpoint, the server responds with the message Hello, World!.
- The app.listen() method starts the server and makes it listen on port 3000.

6. **Run the Server**: In your terminal, run the following command to start your server:

bash

node index.js

Now, open your browser or use a tool like Postman and navigate to http://localhost:3000. You should see the response: Hello, World!.

---

2. Handling GET Requests and Sending Responses

In the example above, you created a simple GET route that responds with a message. Let's explore how GET requests and responses work in more detail.

- **GET Requests**: These are used to retrieve data from the server. In RESTful APIs, GET requests are typically used to read information.
- **Sending Responses**: The res.send() method sends a response back to the client. You can send a variety of response types, such as plain text, JSON, or HTML.

Handling Parameters and Query Strings

You can also handle dynamic parts of the route (such as IDs or query parameters) by using placeholders in the route definition.

Example: Handling a Route Parameter

Let's modify the API to respond with a personalized greeting based on a name provided in the URL.

javascript

```javascript
app.get('/:name', (req, res) => {
  const name = req.params.name;
  res.send(`Hello, ${name}!`);
});
```

- **Explanation**: In this route, :name is a route parameter. When a request is made to http://localhost:3000/John, the server will respond with Hello, John!.

Example: Handling Query Parameters

Query parameters are commonly used to send additional data in GET requests, like filters or search terms.

For example, to send a query parameter for a user's age:

javascript

```javascript
app.get('/greet', (req, res) => {
  const name = req.query.name || 'Stranger';
  const age = req.query.age || 'unknown';
  res.send(`Hello, ${name}. You are ${age} years old.`);
});
```

- **Example URL**: http://localhost:3000/greet?name=John&age=30

- **Response**: Hello, John. You are 30 years old.

---

3. Structuring API Routes

As your API grows, it's important to organize your routes logically. You can structure your API routes in multiple ways. One common approach is to group related routes into separate files or modules, which helps keep your application maintainable and scalable.

Creating Modular Routes

Instead of putting all routes in a single file, you can break them down into separate route modules.

1. **Create a new folder called routes**:

   bash

   mkdir routes

2. **Create a file called greeting.js inside the routes folder**:

   javascript

```javascript
const express = require('express');
const router = express.Router();

// Define a route for the root path
router.get('/', (req, res) => {
    res.send('Hello, World!');
```

```
});
```

```
// Define a route with a dynamic name parameter
router.get('/:name', (req, res) => {
   const name = req.params.name;
   res.send(`Hello, ${name}!`);
});
```

```
// Define a route that uses query parameters
router.get('/greet', (req, res) => {
   const name = req.query.name || 'Stranger';
   const age = req.query.age || 'unknown';
   res.send(`Hello, ${name}. You are ${age} years old.`);
});
```

```
module.exports = router;
```

3. **Modify your index.js to use this new route module**:

javascript

```
const express = require('express');
const app = express();
const greetingRoute = require('./routes/greeting'); // Import the greeting route module
```

```
// Use the greeting route
app.use('/greet', greetingRoute);
```

```
// Start the server
```

```
const PORT = 3000;
app.listen(PORT, () => {
    console.log(`Server running at http://localhost:${PORT}`);
});
```

Now, your API is structured in a way that makes it easier to manage as you add more features.

In this chapter, you've learned how to set up a simple API using Node.js and Express. You've built a basic "Hello World" API and handled GET requests to send back dynamic responses. We also explored how to handle URL parameters and query parameters to make your API more flexible. Lastly, you learned how to structure your API by modularizing your routes for scalability.

As you continue, these foundational concepts will serve as the building blocks for creating more advanced and feature-rich APIs. In the next chapter, we'll dive deeper into handling POST requests and processing incoming data.

Chapter 7: Handling HTTP Methods

In this chapter, we will explore the four primary HTTP methods used to interact with a RESTful API: **GET**, **POST**, **PUT**, and **DELETE**. These methods form the backbone of any RESTful service, allowing clients to perform CRUD (Create, Read, Update, Delete) operations on the resources exposed by the API.

We'll also dive into how to handle errors properly and return the appropriate HTTP status codes, ensuring your API responds correctly in different situations.

By the end of this chapter, you will have a solid understanding of how to handle different HTTP methods and how to structure your API routes to manage data effectively.

1. Working with GET, POST, PUT, and DELETE

HTTP methods allow clients to interact with resources on the server. Here's an overview of how each of these methods is typically used in a RESTful API:

- **GET**: Retrieve data from the server.
- **POST**: Create a new resource on the server.
- **PUT**: Update an existing resource on the server.
- **DELETE**: Remove a resource from the server.

Let's look at each method in more detail, including how to handle them in your Express.js API.

GET: Retrieving Data

The **GET** method is used to request data from the server. It is the most commonly used HTTP method and is generally used to fetch information about a resource without modifying it.

Real-World Example:

- **Fetching all users from a database**
- **Retrieving a list of products in an e-commerce store**
- **Getting weather data from a weather API**

Code Example: Handling GET Requests

Let's start by setting up a route to retrieve data.

javascript

```
// GET route to fetch all users
app.get('/users', (req, res) => {
    const users = [
        { id: 1, name: 'Alice' },
        { id: 2, name: 'Bob' },
    ];
    res.status(200).json(users);  // Send back the list of users as a JSON response
});
```

Here, we defined a route that listens for **GET** requests on /users. When a request is made to this endpoint, we return a JSON array of user objects.

POST: Creating Data

The **POST** method is used to send data to the server to create a new resource. This method is often used for submitting form data or sending data for creation.

Real-World Example:

- **Creating a new user in a database**
- **Submitting a new product to an e-commerce site**
- **Posting a message to a social media feed**

Code Example: Handling POST Requests

Now let's create an endpoint that allows clients to add new users.

javascript

```
// POST route to add a new user
app.post('/users', (req, res) => {
    const newUser = req.body;  // Get data sent in the request body
    newUser.id = Date.now();  // Assign a new ID based on the current timestamp
    users.push(newUser);  // Add the new user to the list
    res.status(201).json(newUser);  // Respond with the newly created user
});
```

In this example:

- We use **req.body** to get the data sent in the request (usually in JSON format).
- The new user is added to the users array, and we return the created user along with a **201 Created** status code, which indicates successful resource creation.

PUT: Updating Data

The **PUT** method is used to update an existing resource. When a PUT request is made, the resource is entirely replaced with the new data provided. If you only want to partially update a resource, consider using the **PATCH** method (which we'll cover later).

Real-World Example:

- **Updating a user's profile**
- **Changing the details of an existing product**
- **Modifying a comment on a blog post**

Code Example: Handling PUT Requests

Let's create a route that allows clients to update a user's information.

javascript

```
// PUT route to update an existing user
```

```
app.put('/users/:id', (req, res) => {
    const userId = parseInt(req.params.id);
    const updatedData = req.body;

    const userIndex = users.findIndex(user => user.id === userId);
    if (userIndex === -1) {
        return res.status(404).json({ message: 'User not found' });
    }

    users[userIndex] = { ...users[userIndex], ...updatedData };  // Update user data
    res.status(200).json(users[userIndex]);  // Return the updated user
});
```

Here's how it works:

- **req.params.id** retrieves the id parameter from the URL (e.g., /users/1).
- We search for the user with that ID, and if the user is found, we update the user's data with the values from **req.body**.

We respond with a **200 OK** status if the update is successful, or a **404 Not Found** if the user doesn't exist.

DELETE: Removing Data

The **DELETE** method is used to remove a resource from the server. This method doesn't require a body, and the resource is simply removed based on the provided identifier.

Real-World Example:

- **Deleting a user from a database**
- **Removing a product from an e-commerce store**
- **Deleting a post from a blog**

Code Example: Handling DELETE Requests

Let's add a route to delete a user by their ID.

javascript

```
// DELETE route to remove a user
app.delete('/users/:id', (req, res) => {
  const userId = parseInt(req.params.id);
  const userIndex = users.findIndex(user => user.id === userId);

  if (userIndex === -1) {
    return res.status(404).json({ message: 'User not found' });
  }

  users.splice(userIndex, 1);  // Remove the user from the array
  res.status(204).send();  // Respond with no content (successful deletion)
});
```

In this example:

- We first find the user by ID.
- If the user exists, we use splice() to remove the user from the users array.

- We respond with a **204 No Content** status, which indicates that the request was successful, but there is no content in the response body.

---

2. Handling Errors with Appropriate HTTP Status Codes

A key part of building APIs is handling errors properly and returning the appropriate HTTP status codes. These status codes provide clients with important information about the success or failure of their requests.

Here are some common HTTP status codes you'll use in your API:

- **200 OK**: The request was successful.
- **201 Created**: The request was successful, and a resource was created.
- **400 Bad Request**: The request was malformed or missing required parameters.
- **404 Not Found**: The resource was not found.
- **500 Internal Server Error**: There was an error on the server side.

You can handle errors by returning these status codes along with an error message that explains the issue.

Example: Handling a Bad Request

javascript

```javascript
app.post('/users', (req, res) => {
  if (!req.body.name || !req.body.age) {
    return res.status(400).json({ message: 'Name and age are required' });
  }
  // Process the request if data is valid
});
```

Here, we return a **400 Bad Request** status if the name or age fields are missing from the request body.

In this chapter, you've learned how to handle the four main HTTP methods: **GET, POST, PUT**, and **DELETE**. Each method serves a specific purpose in managing resources and allows clients to interact with your API effectively. You've also learned how to handle errors and return appropriate HTTP status codes, ensuring that your API responds correctly in various situations.

By understanding and implementing these HTTP methods and status codes, you'll be able to build APIs that are intuitive, efficient, and easy for developers to use.

Chapter 8: Working with JSON Data

In this chapter, we'll explore **JSON** (JavaScript Object Notation), the most widely used data format for exchanging data between clients and servers in modern web applications. JSON is a lightweight, human-readable format that is easy to parse and generate. It has become the de facto standard for representing structured data in RESTful APIs due to its simplicity and versatility.

We'll cover how to send and receive JSON data in requests and responses, and walk through an example of building a simple **JSON-based REST API** for managing user data.

1. Understanding JSON and Why It's the Most Common Data Format in APIs

JSON stands for JavaScript Object Notation. It is a simple, text-based data format that is used to represent structured data, primarily consisting of key-value pairs and ordered lists. JSON is language-agnostic but closely resembles JavaScript object notation, making it a natural fit for web development.

The key features of JSON are:

- **Human-readable**: It's easy to read and write, even for people who are not familiar with programming.
- **Lightweight**: JSON uses minimal syntax, which makes it compact and fast to transmit over the web.
- **Flexible**: It supports arrays, objects, and different data types (strings, numbers, booleans, etc.).
- **Compatible with web technologies**: JSON can be easily processed by JavaScript in the browser and by many other programming languages.

JSON's ability to integrate seamlessly with JavaScript is one of the primary reasons why it is the preferred data format for web applications and APIs.

JSON Structure:

A JSON object is written as a collection of key-value pairs, similar to a JavaScript object. It's enclosed within curly braces {}. A JSON array, which holds ordered lists of values, is enclosed in square brackets [].

Example JSON object:

json

```
{
  "id": 1,
  "name": "John Doe",
  "email": "john.doe@example.com",
```

```
 "active": true
}
```

Example JSON array:

json

```json
[
  { "id": 1, "name": "John Doe" },
  { "id": 2, "name": "Jane Smith" }
]
```

2. Sending and Receiving JSON Data in Requests and Responses

When building APIs, **JSON** is commonly used to send data between the client and the server. In a typical RESTful API workflow, the client (e.g., a web browser or mobile app) sends data to the server in the form of a **JSON payload**. The server processes the request and responds with a **JSON response**.

Sending JSON Data in a Request (Client-Side)
When making API requests, especially **POST**, **PUT**, or **PATCH** requests, you often need to send data to the server. This data is usually sent in the **body** of the request as a JSON object.

Example using Postman or JavaScript (fetch API):

javascript

```
const data = {
  name: 'John Doe',
  email: 'john.doe@example.com',
  active: true
};


fetch('https://yourapi.com/users', {
  method: 'POST',
  headers: {
    'Content-Type': 'application/json'
  },
  body: JSON.stringify(data) // Send the JSON data in the request body
})
  .then(response => response.json())
  .then(data => console.log('User created:', data))
  .catch(error => console.error('Error:', error));
```

In this example:

- We use the **fetch()** method to send a **POST** request to an API endpoint.
- The **Content-Type: application/json** header tells the server that the body contains JSON data.
- The **JSON.stringify(data)** method converts the JavaScript object into a JSON string for transmission.

Receiving JSON Data in the Response (Server-Side)

When a client makes a request to an API, the server typically responds with a JSON object containing the requested data or the result of an operation.

Example using Express.js to return JSON data:

javascript

```
// GET route to fetch a list of users
app.get('/users', (req, res) => {
    const users = [
        { id: 1, name: 'John Doe', email: 'john.doe@example.com', active: true },
        { id: 2, name: 'Jane Smith', email: 'jane.smith@example.com', active: false
}
    ];
    res.json(users);  // Send the users as a JSON response
});
```

In this example:

- The server sends back a JSON array containing user data. The **res.json()** method is used to automatically set the **Content-Type** header to **application/json** and convert the JavaScript object into a JSON string.

---

3. Example: Building a JSON-based REST API for Managing Users

Now, let's build a simple JSON-based REST API using **Node.js** and **Express.js** to manage user data. This API will support basic CRUD operations (Create, Read, Update, Delete) using JSON.

Step 1: Set Up the Express Application

Start by initializing a Node.js project and installing the necessary dependencies:

bash

```
mkdir user-api
cd user-api
npm init -y
npm install express
```

Then, create a file called **app.js** to set up the basic Express server.

javascript

```
const express = require('express');
const app = express();

// Middleware to parse JSON bodies
app.use(express.json());

const users = [
  { id: 1, name: 'Alice', email: 'alice@example.com' },
  { id: 2, name: 'Bob', email: 'bob@example.com' }
];

// Route to get all users
```

```
app.get('/users', (req, res) => {
  res.status(200).json(users);
});

// Route to create a new user
app.post('/users', (req, res) => {
  const newUser = req.body;
  newUser.id = users.length + 1;
  users.push(newUser);
  res.status(201).json(newUser);
});

// Route to update a user
app.put('/users/:id', (req, res) => {
  const userId = parseInt(req.params.id);
  const updatedData = req.body;

  const userIndex = users.findIndex(user => user.id === userId);
  if (userIndex === -1) {
    return res.status(404).json({ message: 'User not found' });
  }

  users[userIndex] = { ...users[userIndex], ...updatedData };
  res.status(200).json(users[userIndex]);
});

// Route to delete a user
app.delete('/users/:id', (req, res) => {
  const userId = parseInt(req.params.id);
  const userIndex = users.findIndex(user => user.id === userId);
```

```
if (userIndex === -1) {
  return res.status(404).json({ message: 'User not found' });
}

users.splice(userIndex, 1);
res.status(204).send(); // No content to return
});

const port = 3000;
app.listen(port, () => {
  console.log(`Server is running on http://localhost:${port}`);
});
```

Step 2: Test the API

With this setup, you now have the following endpoints:

1. **GET /users**: Retrieve all users in JSON format.
2. **POST /users**: Add a new user by sending a JSON object in the request body.
3. **PUT /users/:id**: Update a user's information by sending a JSON object.
4. **DELETE /users/:id**: Remove a user by ID.

You can test the API using **Postman** or directly with curl commands to send **GET**, **POST**, **PUT**, and **DELETE** requests.

In this chapter, we've learned about JSON, the most common data format for APIs, and how it is used to send and receive data in a RESTful API. We've also built a simple user management API that handles JSON data for creating, retrieving, updating, and deleting user records.

Mastering JSON and understanding how to handle it effectively in your API is essential for building modern web applications. In the next chapters, we'll continue to explore more advanced features and best practices for creating robust APIs with Node.js and Express.

Chapter 9: Handling Middleware in Express

In this chapter, we will dive into **middleware** in Express.js, which is a powerful concept for building flexible and scalable APIs. Middleware functions allow us to run code during the request-response cycle, making them essential for tasks like logging, authentication, error handling, and more.

Middleware plays a key role in ensuring that your API can handle requests efficiently and securely. We will explore how to use built-in middleware functions, as well as how to create custom middleware to enhance the functionality of your API.

1. What is Middleware in Express?

Middleware in Express is any function that is executed during the lifecycle of a request. It sits between the incoming request and the final response that is sent back to the client. Middleware can be used to perform a wide range of tasks, such as:

- Modifying the request or response objects
- Executing code (such as logging or authentication)
- Ending the request-response cycle or passing control to the next middleware in the chain

Middleware is a function that takes three parameters:

javascript

```
function (req, res, next) {
  // middleware logic here
}
```

- **req**: The request object, representing the incoming HTTP request.
- **res**: The response object, representing the outgoing HTTP response.
- **next**: A function that, when called, passes control to the next middleware function.

Middleware functions are executed in the order they are added to the Express app, making the order of middleware important.

---

2. Built-in Middleware in Express

Express comes with several built-in middleware functions that are commonly used in web applications. Let's explore some of the most essential ones:

express.json()

The **express.json()** middleware is used to parse incoming requests with JSON payloads. This is especially useful when you're building RESTful APIs that expect to receive JSON data in the request body (such as when creating or updating resources).

Example:

javascript

```
const express = require('express');
const app = express();

// Built-in middleware to parse JSON bodies
app.use(express.json());

// Example POST route
app.post('/users', (req, res) => {
  const user = req.body;  // Accessing the parsed JSON data
  console.log(user);
  res.status(201).json({ message: 'User created successfully', user });
});
```

In this example:

- The **express.json()** middleware automatically parses incoming JSON requests and makes the parsed data available in req.body.

express.static()

The **express.static()** middleware serves static files like HTML, CSS, JavaScript, and images directly from the server. It's used to serve files from a specific directory in your project.

Example:

javascript

```
// Serve static files from the 'public' folder
app.use(express.static('public'));
```

This code tells Express to serve files in the public directory as static assets. For example, if you place an index.html file in the public folder, it will be accessible at http://localhost:3000/index.html.

---

3. Writing Custom Middleware for Logging, Authentication, etc.

While Express provides many built-in middleware functions, you can also write your own custom middleware to handle tasks specific to your API. Let's explore how to create custom middleware for common tasks like logging, authentication, and error handling.

Logging Middleware

A common use case for middleware is to log details about incoming requests, such as the HTTP method, the URL, and the request timestamp. This is useful for debugging and monitoring purposes.

Example:

javascript

```javascript
// Custom logging middleware
function logRequest(req, res, next) {
  console.log(`${req.method} request to ${req.url} at ${new Date().toISOString()}`);
  next(); // Pass control to the next middleware
}
```

```javascript
// Use logging middleware globally
app.use(logRequest);
```

This middleware logs information about every incoming request. The **next()** function ensures that the request continues to the next middleware in the stack.

Authentication Middleware

For API security, it's often necessary to authenticate users before they can access certain routes. You can create middleware that checks for the presence of an authorization token and validates it.

Example:

javascript

```javascript
function authenticate(req, res, next) {
  const token = req.headers['authorization'];

  if (!token) {
    return res.status(401).json({ message: 'Authentication required' });
  }
```

```
// Simulate token validation (you can replace this with real token logic)
if (token === 'valid-token') {
  next();  // Token is valid, pass control to the next middleware
} else {
  res.status(403).json({ message: 'Invalid token' });
}
}
```

```
// Apply authentication middleware to specific routes
app.use('/protected', authenticate);
```

In this example:

- The **authenticate()** middleware checks if the request has an **Authorization header** with a valid token.
- If the token is missing or invalid, it returns a 401 (Unauthorized) or 403 (Forbidden) response, respectively.
- If the token is valid, it calls **next()** to allow the request to proceed.

You can apply this middleware to specific routes (e.g., '/protected'), which ensures that only authenticated users can access them.

Error Handling Middleware

Error handling is another important use of middleware. Custom error-handling middleware can catch errors that occur during the request-response cycle and provide a standardized error response.

Example:

javascript

```
// Error-handling middleware (must be defined last)
app.use((err, req, res, next) => {
  console.error(err.stack);  // Log the error stack trace
  res.status(500).json({ message: 'Something went wrong!', error: err.message });
});
```

In this example:

- The error-handling middleware takes four arguments: **err, req, res,** and **next.**
- If an error occurs anywhere in the middleware stack, this handler will catch it and return a **500 (Internal Server Error)** response with the error message.
- The **console.error()** function logs the error stack trace for debugging purposes.

---

4. Chaining Middleware Functions

One of the strengths of Express is its ability to chain multiple middleware functions together. Middleware can be applied globally to all routes or to specific routes, allowing you to build flexible and modular APIs.

Example of chaining middleware functions:

javascript

```
app.use(logRequest);  // Log every request

// Apply the authentication middleware to specific routes
app.use('/protected', authenticate);

// Define routes
app.get('/protected/data', (req, res) => {
  res.json({ message: 'This is protected data' });
});
```

In this example:

- The **logRequest** middleware logs every request.
- The **authenticate** middleware is applied only to routes under **/protected**. If the authentication fails, users cannot access the route.

5.

Middleware is a powerful feature in Express that allows you to build modular, flexible, and scalable APIs. By leveraging built-in middleware, such as **express.json()** and **express.static()**, and writing custom middleware for tasks like logging, authentication, and error handling, you can create a more secure and maintainable API.

In the next chapters, we will build on the knowledge gained from this chapter to develop more advanced features for your API, including handling data validation, managing user sessions, and integrating with third-party services.

Chapter 10: Validating Data and Error Handling

In this chapter, we will focus on **validating incoming data** and **handling errors** in your Express.js API. Data validation is crucial for ensuring that the information sent to your API is in the correct format, and error handling ensures that your API responds appropriately to issues during the request-response cycle. Together, these two techniques improve the reliability and security of your API.

---

1. Using express-validator for Data Validation

In any real-world API, you'll often need to ensure that incoming data is valid before processing it. This is especially important for requests that involve user input, like when users create or update resources. To handle this, we can use **express-validator**, a popular library for data validation in Express.js.

What is express-validator?

express-validator is a set of middleware functions that allow you to validate and sanitize incoming request data (query parameters, request body, headers, etc.). It helps to check if data meets certain criteria (e.g., a field is required, a value is of a specific type, or a string matches a certain pattern).

Installing express-validator

You can install express-validator using npm:

bash

npm install express-validator

Validating Request Data

To validate incoming data, you use the check() function provided by express-validator. The check() function validates a field in the request body, query parameters, or URL parameters based on the specified rules.

For example, let's validate data from a user registration form that requires a valid email, a minimum password length, and a username that is at least 3 characters long.

javascript

```
const { check, validationResult } = require('express-validator');

// Validation middleware for user registration
app.post('/register', [
  check('email').isEmail().withMessage('Please enter a valid email'),
  check('password').isLength({ min: 6 }).withMessage('Password must be at
least 6 characters long'),
```

```
check('username').isLength({ min: 3 }).withMessage('Username must be at
least 3 characters long'),
], (req, res) => {
  // Extract validation errors
  const errors = validationResult(req);

  if (!errors.isEmpty()) {
    // If validation fails, return the errors
    return res.status(400).json({ errors: errors.array() });
  }

  // If validation passes, proceed with registration logic
  const { email, password, username } = req.body;
  res.status(201).json({ message: 'User registered successfully', data: { email,
username } });
});
```

In this example:

- The **check()** function validates the fields **email, password,** and **username**.
- The **isEmail()** function checks if the email is in a valid format.
- The **isLength()** function checks the length of the password and username.
- The **validationResult()** function is used to extract any validation errors, which are then returned in the response if validation fails.

2. Handling Validation Errors and Sending Appropriate Responses

When validation fails, it's important to send clear and helpful error messages back to the client. The **validationResult()** function in express-validator will collect all errors from the validation process. If any errors are found, you should send a **400 Bad Request** response, which indicates that the request was malformed and cannot be processed.

Example of sending validation error responses:

javascript

```
app.post('/login', [
  check('username').isAlphanumeric().withMessage('Username    must    only
contain letters and numbers'),
  check('password').notEmpty().withMessage('Password is required')
], (req, res) => {
  const errors = validationResult(req);

  if (!errors.isEmpty()) {
    return res.status(400).json({ errors: errors.array() });
  }

  // Proceed with login logic
  res.status(200).json({ message: 'Login successful' });
});
```

In this case:

- If the **username** is not alphanumeric or the **password** is empty, validation will fail, and a **400 status code** will be returned with an array of error messages.
- This helps the client understand what went wrong and what needs to be corrected.

---

3. Proper Error Handling with Try-Catch Blocks and Custom Error Messages

In addition to data validation, error handling is an essential part of building robust APIs. Errors can occur for many reasons, such as database issues, missing dependencies, or unexpected exceptions. Handling these errors gracefully will ensure that your API provides meaningful feedback and doesn't crash.

Try-Catch Blocks for Synchronous Code

For synchronous code, you can use **try-catch blocks** to catch exceptions and handle errors appropriately.

Example:

javascript

```
app.get('/user/:id', (req, res) => {
  try {
    const userId = req.params.id;
```

```
const user = getUserFromDatabase(userId);  // Simulated function to fetch a user

if (!user) {
  throw new Error('User not found');
}

res.status(200).json({ user });
} catch (err) {
res.status(500).json({ message: err.message });
}
});
```

In this example:

- We try to retrieve a user from the database.
- If the user is not found, an error is thrown, and it is caught in the **catch** block.
- A **500 status code** is returned, indicating a server error, along with a message detailing the error.

Async/Await and Try-Catch Blocks

When working with asynchronous code, such as database queries or API calls, you can use **async/await** along with **try-catch** to handle errors.

Example with asynchronous database query:

javascript

```
app.post('/create-user', async (req, res) => {
  try {
    const { username, email } = req.body;
    const user = await createUserInDatabase(username, email);   // Async DB
operation
    res.status(201).json({ message: 'User created successfully', user });
  } catch (err) {
    res.status(500).json({ message: 'Internal server error: ' + err.message });
  }
});
```

In this case:

- The **createUserInDatabase()** function returns a promise that resolves when the user is successfully created.
- If something goes wrong during this process (e.g., a database issue), the error is caught, and a **500 status code** is returned with the error message.

Custom Error Handling Middleware

For a more organized approach, you can create a **custom error-handling middleware** that catches all errors in your application and formats the response consistently.

Example of a custom error handler:

javascript

```
// Custom error-handling middleware (must be defined after routes)
app.use((err, req, res, next) => {
```

```
console.error(err.stack);  // Log the full error for debugging
res.status(err.status || 500).json({
  message: err.message || 'Something went wrong!',
  error: process.env.NODE_ENV === 'production' ? {} : err
 });
});
```

This middleware:

- Catches all errors passed via the **next()** function.
- Logs the error stack for debugging purposes (in development environments).
- Sends a structured error response with a message and status code.

4.

In this chapter, we've learned how to handle data validation and errors in your Express.js API. **express-validator** makes it easy to validate incoming data, ensuring that requests meet specific requirements before processing them. Furthermore, error handling with **try-catch blocks** and **custom error-handling middleware** ensures that your API provides helpful feedback and doesn't crash unexpectedly.

By incorporating proper data validation and error handling, you can make your API more reliable, secure, and user-friendly, providing a better experience for both developers and users interacting with your system.

Chapter 11: Creating a Dynamic API with MongoDB

In this chapter, we will focus on integrating **MongoDB** with your Node.js application to build a dynamic and data-driven API. **MongoDB** is a popular NoSQL database that stores data in a flexible, JSON-like format called BSON (Binary JSON). It allows for the storage of complex data structures and is well-suited for scalable applications. We will also use **Mongoose**, a powerful Object Data Modeling (ODM) library for MongoDB, which simplifies data interactions with MongoDB by providing a higher-level abstraction.

---

1. Introduction to MongoDB and Mongoose

What is MongoDB?

MongoDB is a **NoSQL database** that stores data in a flexible, schema-less format. Unlike traditional relational databases, MongoDB uses collections and documents to store data, which means it doesn't require a fixed schema. This allows for rapid development and scaling of applications as the data model can change easily without causing major disruptions.

MongoDB's key features include:

- **Flexible Schema**: You can store data without predefined schemas.
- **Scalable**: MongoDB supports horizontal scaling by distributing data across multiple servers.
- **Fast Reads and Writes**: MongoDB is designed to be high-performance, particularly for read-heavy workloads.

What is Mongoose?

Mongoose is an ODM (Object Data Modeling) library for **MongoDB** and **Node.js**. It provides a higher-level abstraction over MongoDB, allowing you to define models with schemas, and perform database operations with a more intuitive API. Mongoose makes it easier to work with MongoDB by providing built-in methods for querying, validation, and data manipulation.

---

2. Setting Up MongoDB in Node.js

To begin using MongoDB with Node.js, you'll need to install MongoDB and Mongoose, and set up a basic connection to the database.

Installing MongoDB and Mongoose

- If you don't already have **MongoDB** installed, you can either use a local installation or a cloud-based MongoDB service like MongoDB Atlas.

- Install **Mongoose** via npm:

bash

npm install mongoose

Setting Up a MongoDB Database

To interact with MongoDB, you'll need to set up a connection. You can connect to a local MongoDB instance or a cloud-based instance like MongoDB Atlas.

Here's how to connect to a local MongoDB instance:

javascript

```javascript
const mongoose = require('mongoose');

// Connect to the local MongoDB instance
mongoose.connect('mongodb://localhost/myDatabase', { useNewUrlParser: true,
useUnifiedTopology: true })
  .then(() => {
    console.log('Connected to MongoDB');
  })
  .catch(err => {
    console.error('Connection error', err);
  });
```

For a cloud-based MongoDB instance (such as MongoDB Atlas), you will need a connection string provided by MongoDB Atlas, which you can find in the "Clusters" section of the Atlas dashboard.

Using MongoDB Atlas for Cloud Hosting

If you're using MongoDB Atlas, you can obtain your connection string from the Atlas UI. The connection string will look something like this:

plaintext

```
mongodb+srv://<username>:<password>@cluster0.mongodb.net/<dbname>?retryWrites=true&w=majority
```

Replace <username>, <password>, and <dbname> with your MongoDB Atlas credentials and database name.

---

3. Creating, Reading, Updating, and Deleting Data with MongoDB

In this section, we'll walk through the basic CRUD (Create, Read, Update, Delete) operations using MongoDB and Mongoose.

Creating Data (Create)

To create data in MongoDB, you first define a **Mongoose model** with a schema that specifies the structure of the data.

Here's how you define a basic **User** schema with Mongoose:

javascript

```javascript
const mongoose = require('mongoose');
```

```
// Define a User schema
const userSchema = new mongoose.Schema({
  name: { type: String, required: true },
  email: { type: String, required: true, unique: true },
  age: { type: Number, required: true }
});

// Create a model from the schema
const User = mongoose.model('User', userSchema);

// Create a new user
const newUser = new User({
  name: 'John Doe',
  email: 'john.doe@example.com',
  age: 30
});

// Save the new user to the database
newUser.save()
  .then(() => console.log('User saved successfully'))
  .catch(err => console.error('Error saving user:', err));
```

In this example:

- A **User** schema is defined with name, email, and age fields.
- The **save()** method is used to create a new user and store it in the database.

Reading Data (Read)

To retrieve data from MongoDB, you can use the **find()** method to search for documents that match specific criteria.

Example of reading all users:

javascript

```
User.find()
 .then(users => {
   console.log('All users:', users);
 })
 .catch(err => console.error('Error retrieving users:', err));
```

Example of reading a single user by ID:

javascript

```
const userId = '605c72ef9e1d4b1b4b9f69a2';  // Replace with an actual user ID

User.findById(userId)
 .then(user => {
   if (!user) {
     console.log('User not found');
   } else {
     console.log('User found:', user);
   }
 })
 .catch(err => console.error('Error retrieving user:', err));
```

Here:

- **find()** retrieves all users from the database.

- **findById()** retrieves a single user by their unique ID.

Updating Data (Update)

To update an existing document, you can use the **updateOne()** or **findByIdAndUpdate()** method.

Example of updating a user's age:

javascript

```
const userId = '605c72ef9e1d4b1b4b9f69a2'; // Replace with an actual user ID
const newAge = 31;

User.findByIdAndUpdate(userId, { age: newAge }, { new: true })
  .then(updatedUser => {
    console.log('Updated user:', updatedUser);
})
  .catch(err => console.error('Error updating user:', err));
```

Here:

- **findByIdAndUpdate()** finds a user by ID and updates their age field to the new value. The { new: true } option ensures that the updated document is returned.

Deleting Data (Delete)

To delete a document, use the **deleteOne()** or **findByIdAndDelete()** method.

Example of deleting a user:

javascript

```
const userId = '605c72ef9e1d4b1b4b9f69a2';  // Replace with an actual user ID

User.findByIdAndDelete(userId)
  .then(() => {
    console.log('User deleted successfully');
  })
  .catch(err => console.error('Error deleting user:', err));
```

In this example:

- **findByIdAndDelete()** removes a user from the database by their ID.

In this chapter, we've learned how to set up MongoDB and Mongoose with Node.js, and how to perform basic CRUD operations: **Create**, **Read**, **Update**, and **Delete**. By using MongoDB's flexible NoSQL structure and Mongoose's powerful ODM, you can easily build and manage dynamic APIs. These capabilities provide a strong foundation for building more complex, data-driven applications. In future chapters, we will explore additional API features like authentication, validation, and optimization, further enhancing your API development skills.

Chapter 12: Integrating with a Database: SQL vs NoSQL

In this chapter, we will explore the differences between SQL and NoSQL databases and discuss when to use each type for building your API. We will also look at how to integrate both types of databases with your **Node.js** API. Databases are at the core of dynamic applications and understanding when to use the right type of database is key to building efficient and scalable APIs.

1. Understanding the Differences Between SQL and NoSQL Databases

What is a SQL Database?

SQL (Structured Query Language) databases are **relational databases** that store data in a structured format using tables with predefined schemas. These tables consist of rows and columns, and each column has a specific data type. SQL databases are ideal for handling structured data with well-defined relationships between entities.

Common SQL databases include:

- **MySQL**
- **PostgreSQL**

- **SQLite**
- **Microsoft SQL Server**

Key Characteristics of SQL Databases:

- **Schema-based**: SQL databases require a predefined schema to define the structure of data (e.g., tables, columns, constraints).
- **ACID Compliance**: SQL databases follow ACID principles (Atomicity, Consistency, Isolation, Durability), ensuring reliable transactions.
- **Table-based**: Data is stored in tables, and relationships are typically established via foreign keys.

What is a NoSQL Database?

NoSQL (Not Only SQL) databases are non-relational databases designed for flexibility, scalability, and handling unstructured or semi-structured data. NoSQL databases store data in formats like key-value pairs, documents, wide-column stores, or graphs.

Common NoSQL databases include:

- **MongoDB** (Document-based)
- **Cassandra** (Column-family based)
- **Redis** (Key-value store)
- **CouchDB** (Document-based)
- **Neo4j** (Graph-based)

Key Characteristics of NoSQL Databases:

- **Schema-less**: NoSQL databases often don't require a fixed schema, making them ideal for rapidly changing or dynamic data.
- **Scalability**: NoSQL databases are designed to scale horizontally, meaning they can easily distribute data across many servers.
- **Flexible Data Models**: Data can be stored in various formats, such as JSON, BSON, or key-value pairs.

Key Differences Between SQL and NoSQL Databases:

Feature	SQL Databases	NoSQL Databases
Data Structure	Structured (Tables, Rows, Columns)	Unstructured or Semi-structured (JSON, Key-Value, Graphs, etc.)
Schema	Fixed Schema (predefined tables and columns)	Flexible Schema (no fixed structure)
Scalability	Vertical scaling (more powerful servers)	Horizontal scaling (distribute across many servers)
Transactions	ACID compliance	Eventual consistency

Feature	SQL Databases	NoSQL Databases
	(strong consistency)	(depending on type)
Best Use Case	Structured data with complex relationships	Flexible, large-scale data with rapid changes or high volume

2. When to Use SQL vs NoSQL for Your API

When to Use SQL Databases

- **Structured Data**: When your data has a predefined structure and fits well into tables with rows and columns.
- **ACID Transactions**: If your application requires strong consistency and reliable transaction support (e.g., banking, financial services).
- **Complex Relationships**: If your data has complex relationships, such as foreign keys, and you need to perform JOIN operations (e.g., customer orders, user profiles).
- **Reporting and Analytics**: SQL databases are well-suited for analytical queries and reporting, as they can easily handle complex joins, grouping, and aggregation.

Use Case Examples:

- E-commerce platforms (customer data, orders, products, etc.)
- Financial applications (transactions, accounts, auditing)
- Inventory management systems

When to Use NoSQL Databases

- **Unstructured or Semi-structured Data**: When your data is dynamic or doesn't fit well into a relational schema (e.g., user-generated content, sensor data, log files).
- **Horizontal Scalability**: If you need to scale out easily to handle large amounts of data across multiple servers (e.g., large web applications or IoT systems).
- **Rapid Development**: NoSQL databases are useful when the data model is expected to evolve frequently or rapidly, especially during early development stages.
- **High Availability**: NoSQL databases are often designed for fault-tolerance and high availability, making them ideal for distributed systems with a large user base.

Use Case Examples:

- Social media applications (comments, likes, and posts)
- Content management systems (blogs, media libraries)
- IoT systems (devices sending large volumes of data)
- Real-time analytics platforms

3. Integrating an SQL Database (e.g., PostgreSQL, MySQL) with Your Node.js API

In this section, we will walk through integrating an **SQL database** into your Node.js API. We will use **PostgreSQL** as an example, but the process is similar for other SQL databases like MySQL.

Setting Up PostgreSQL in Node.js

1. **Install PostgreSQL:**
   - You can install PostgreSQL locally or use a cloud-based PostgreSQL service (e.g., Heroku Postgres).
   - To install PostgreSQL locally, visit the official PostgreSQL download page.

2. **Install pg (PostgreSQL client for Node.js):**

   You can interact with PostgreSQL using the pg package in Node.js:

   bash

   ```
   npm install pg
   ```

3. **Create a Database and Table in PostgreSQL:**

Once PostgreSQL is installed, you can create a database and a table for your API. Open the PostgreSQL command line and run:

sql

```
CREATE DATABASE api_db;
\c api_db
```

```
CREATE TABLE users (
  id SERIAL PRIMARY KEY,
  name VARCHAR(100) NOT NULL,
  email VARCHAR(100) NOT NULL UNIQUE
);
```

4. Connecting Node.js to PostgreSQL:

Now, in your Node.js application, you can connect to the PostgreSQL database using the pg module:

javascript

```
const { Client } = require('pg');
```

```
const client = new Client({
  host: 'localhost',
  port: 5432,
  database: 'api_db',
  user: 'your-username',
  password: 'your-password',
```

```
        });
```

```
        client.connect()
          .then(() => console.log('Connected to PostgreSQL'))
          .catch(err => console.error('Error connecting to PostgreSQL', err));
```

Performing CRUD Operations in PostgreSQL

Now, let's go over how to implement **Create**, **Read**, **Update**, and **Delete** operations using PostgreSQL.

Creating Data:

javascript

```javascript
const createUser = async (name, email) => {
  const query = 'INSERT INTO users (name, email) VALUES ($1, $2) RETURNING *';
  const values = [name, email];

  try {
    const result = await client.query(query, values);
    console.log('User created:', result.rows[0]);
  } catch (err) {
    console.error('Error creating user:', err);
  }
};
```

Reading Data:

javascript

```javascript
const getUsers = async () => {
```

```javascript
  const query = 'SELECT * FROM users';

  try {
    const result = await client.query(query);
    console.log('Users:', result.rows);
  } catch (err) {
    console.error('Error retrieving users:', err);
  }
};
```

Updating Data:

javascript

```javascript
const updateUser = async (id, name, email) => {
  const query = 'UPDATE users SET name = $1, email = $2 WHERE id = $3 RETURNING *';
  const values = [name, email, id];

  try {
    const result = await client.query(query, values);
    console.log('Updated user:', result.rows[0]);
  } catch (err) {
    console.error('Error updating user:', err);
  }
};
```

Deleting Data:

javascript

```javascript
const deleteUser = async (id) => {
  const query = 'DELETE FROM users WHERE id = $1 RETURNING *';
```

```
const values = [id];

try {
  const result = await client.query(query, values);
  console.log('Deleted user:', result.rows[0]);
} catch (err) {
  console.error('Error deleting user:', err);
}
};
```

: SQL vs NoSQL for Your API

In this chapter, we have:

- Explored the differences between **SQL** and **NoSQL** databases and when to use each type.
- Walked through integrating a **PostgreSQL** database with a Node.js API using the pg module.
- Discussed basic CRUD operations (Create, Read, Update, Delete) with an SQL database.

Choosing between SQL and NoSQL databases largely depends on the type of data you're working with and the scalability needs of your application. SQL databases are ideal for structured data with complex relationships, while NoSQL databases excel in handling unstructured data and large-scale applications with flexible schema requirements.

In the following chapters, we will continue to build on this foundation by adding more advanced features to your API, including authentication, authorization, and handling data efficiently at scale.

Chapter 13: Introduction to Authentication and Security

In this chapter, we will dive into the concept of **authentication** in the context of API development. Authentication is a critical part of securing your API and ensuring that only authorized users can access your system. We will explore common authentication methods such as **Basic Auth**, **API Keys**, **OAuth**, and **JWT** (JSON Web Tokens). We will also focus on **JWT** as it is one of the most widely used methods for stateless authentication in modern web applications.

---

1. What is Authentication in an API?

Authentication is the process of verifying the identity of a user, application, or service that is trying to access a system. In the context of an **API**, authentication ensures that requests are coming from valid and trusted sources.

Without authentication, anyone can make requests to your API, which could lead to data breaches, unauthorized access, or malicious activities. Thus, authentication is essential for securing APIs, especially in environments that handle sensitive or private information.

When building an API, you need to determine how to verify the identity of the user or service making a request. This is where **authentication methods** come into play.

---

2. Basic Authentication Methods

There are several common ways to authenticate users and applications interacting with your API. Each method has its pros and cons, depending on your API's security requirements.

a. Basic Authentication

Basic Authentication is a simple method where the client sends a username and password with each request. This information is typically included in the HTTP **Authorization header**. While it is easy to implement, it is not very secure because credentials are transmitted in plain text (unless the connection is secured with HTTPS).

How it works:

- The client sends a request with the Authorization header in the format: Basic <Base64-encoded username:password>

Example:

http

Authorization: Basic dXNlcm5hbWU6cGFzc3dvcmQ=

Where the dXNlcm5hbWU6cGFzc3dvcmQ= part is the Base64 encoding of the username and password.

Drawbacks:

- Transmitting credentials on every request increases the risk of exposure (especially on unencrypted connections).
- It is also vulnerable to replay attacks if not used in conjunction with HTTPS.

---

b. API Keys

An **API Key** is a unique identifier that is used to authenticate a client. API keys are usually sent as part of the request header or URL parameters. They are simpler and more secure than Basic Authentication, but they still require additional security measures to prevent unauthorized access, such as restricting access to certain endpoints based on API keys or rotating keys periodically.

How it works:

- The client sends the API key in the request header or as a URL parameter.

Example (in the header):

http

Authorization: ApiKey 123456abcdef

Example (in the URL):

http

GET /data?api_key=123456abcdef

Drawbacks:

- API keys can still be stolen or exposed if not handled securely.
- API keys are not always tied to specific users, so they may lack granularity in terms of access control.

---

c. OAuth (Open Authorization)

OAuth is a more advanced and secure method for authentication and authorization. It is widely used for allowing third-party applications to access a user's data without sharing their credentials directly. OAuth separates the role of authentication (verifying identity) from authorization (granting permissions).

OAuth is typically used when users need to authorize third-party apps to access their data, for example, when you log into an app using your Google or Facebook account.

OAuth works using two main components:

BUILDING APIS WITH NODE.JS

1. **OAuth 2.0**: A framework for granting third-party applications limited access to resources on behalf of the user.
2. **Access Tokens**: After the user authenticates, the system generates an access token that can be used by third-party applications to access protected resources.

How it works:

- A user logs into a service (e.g., Google, Facebook) via OAuth and grants permission for the third-party application to access certain data.
- The API generates an access token, which the third-party app can use to authenticate itself for further requests.

OAuth provides more granular control over what a client can access and when it can access it. It also enables **scopes**, which limit the access level to specific resources.

Drawbacks:

- OAuth can be complex to implement and manage.
- Requires setting up an OAuth provider (e.g., Google or Facebook for social login).

---

d. JWT (JSON Web Tokens)

JSON Web Tokens (JWT) is a popular method for **stateless authentication**. JWTs are compact, URL-safe tokens that can be used to authenticate users and exchange information securely. Unlike traditional session-based authentication, which requires the server to store session information, JWT is stateless, meaning all the information needed to verify the user's identity is embedded in the token itself.

How JWT works:

1. **Login**: A user provides their credentials (e.g., username and password).
2. **Token Generation**: If the credentials are valid, the server generates a JWT containing the user's ID and other claims (e.g., expiration time) and sends it back to the client.
3. **Authentication**: The client includes the JWT in the Authorization header as a Bearer token for every subsequent request.

Example:

http

Authorization: Bearer <JWT-token>

The JWT is typically composed of three parts:

- **Header**: Contains metadata about the token (e.g., type and signing algorithm).

- **Payload**: Contains claims (user data, expiration time, etc.).
- **Signature**: A cryptographic signature to verify the authenticity of the token.

Advantages of JWT:

- **Stateless Authentication**: No need to store session data on the server. The token itself contains all the information.
- **Scalable**: Ideal for distributed and microservices architectures where maintaining sessions would be challenging.
- **Security**: The payload is signed, ensuring it hasn't been tampered with. You can also use encryption for added security.

Drawbacks:

- If a JWT is stolen, it can be used until it expires (unless additional mechanisms like revocation are implemented).
- JWT tokens can become large if they contain a lot of data, which might impact performance.

3. Introduction to Stateless Authentication with JWT

One of the key features of JWT is **stateless authentication**. In traditional session-based authentication, the server stores session information (often in a cookie), and the client sends this session ID with each request. This can lead to scalability issues in distributed systems, as session data must be shared across all servers.

With **JWT**, however, the server does not need to store any session data. Instead, it creates a token that contains the user's identity and any other necessary information, such as access rights or expiration time. The client stores the token (often in local storage or as a cookie) and sends it with every request.

JWT Example in Node.js:
Here's a basic example of how to implement JWT authentication in a **Node.js API** using the **jsonwebtoken** package:

1. **Install the required package**:

    bash

    npm install jsonwebtoken

2. **Creating a JWT after user login**:

    javascript

    ```
    const jwt = require('jsonwebtoken');

    const generateToken = (user) => {
      const payload = {
        id: user.id,
    ```

```
        username: user.username,
    };
    const secret = 'your-secret-key';
    const options = { expiresIn: '1h' };  // Expiry time of 1 hour

    return jwt.sign(payload, secret, options);
};
```

3. Verifying JWT in Subsequent Requests:

javascript

```
const verifyToken = (req, res, next) => {
    const token = req.headers['authorization']?.split(' ')[1];

    if (!token) return res.status(401).send('Access Denied');

    jwt.verify(token, 'your-secret-key', (err, decoded) => {
        if (err) return res.status(403).send('Invalid Token');
        req.user = decoded;
        next();
    });
};
```

4. Securing Routes:

Use the verifyToken middleware to secure your routes:

javascript

```
app.get('/protected', verifyToken, (req, res) => {
```

```
res.json({ message: 'This is a protected route', user: req.user });
});
```

Authentication is crucial in any API to ensure that only authorized users can access certain resources. Understanding the different authentication methods—**Basic Auth, API Keys, OAuth**, and **JWT**—is essential for building secure and scalable APIs. By using **JWT**, you can implement **stateless authentication**, which is particularly useful for modern, distributed applications. In the following chapters, we will continue to build on these concepts, showing you how to implement robust security features in your APIs.

Chapter 14: Building Secure Authentication with JWT

In this chapter, we will focus on building secure authentication in your API using **JWT (JSON Web Tokens)**. JWT provides a scalable and stateless solution for authentication, which is especially useful in modern web applications where multiple microservices and distributed architectures are involved. This chapter will guide you through the steps to set up JWT-based authentication in **Node.js**, create a login system, issue JWT tokens, and protect routes with JWT authentication.

---

1. Setting Up JWT Authentication in Node.js

To begin using JWT for authentication in your Node.js application, you'll need to install the **jsonwebtoken** package, which will allow you to create, verify, and manage JWT tokens.

Step 1: Install the Required Package

In your project directory, open your terminal and install **jsonwebtoken** by running the following command:

bash

```
npm install jsonwebtoken
```

You will also need the **bcryptjs** package to hash user passwords securely, so install it as well:

bash

npm install bcryptjs

Step 2: Set Up the JWT Middleware

Now that the necessary packages are installed, you'll need to set up middleware to generate and verify JWT tokens. First, create a new file named authMiddleware.js to handle the authentication logic:

js

```js
const jwt = require('jsonwebtoken');
const SECRET_KEY = 'yourSecretKey'; // Keep this in an environment variable

// Middleware to verify JWT token
const authenticateToken = (req, res, next) => {
  const token = req.header('Authorization')?.split(' ')[1]; // Extract token from Authorization header
  if (!token) {
    return res.status(403).json({ message: 'Access denied, no token provided' });
  }

  try {
    // Verify the token
    const decoded = jwt.verify(token, SECRET_KEY);
    req.user = decoded; // Add the decoded token to the request object
    next(); // Proceed to the next middleware or route handler
```

```
  } catch (error) {
    res.status(400).json({ message: 'Invalid token' });
  }
};
```

```
module.exports = { authenticateToken };
```

This middleware will:

- Check if the token is provided in the Authorization header.
- Verify the token using the secret key.
- Attach the decoded information (user data) to the request object (req.user) so it can be accessed in the protected routes.

2. Creating a Login System and Issuing JWT Tokens

With JWT authentication set up, the next step is to create a login system. In this system, the user will submit their credentials, and if they are valid, the server will issue a JWT token. The user will then use this token for authentication on subsequent requests.

Step 1: Create the User Login Route

You will need a route to handle user login. Let's create a simple login route in authRoute.js where users can authenticate and receive a JWT token.

Here is how the login system works:

- The user submits their credentials (username and password).
- The server checks the credentials against the database (for the sake of simplicity, let's assume they are stored in an array or database).
- If the credentials are correct, the server will issue a JWT token containing the user's data.

js

```js
const express = require('express');
const bcrypt = require('bcryptjs');
const jwt = require('jsonwebtoken');
const router = express.Router();

// Dummy user data (replace with a real database in production)
const users = [
    {       id:     1,      username:       'user1',        password:
'$2a$10$YFQ0IXtZktt1QbTKYwvWqO0d6U7h8qAwjP5s9hFkB.Nwxtcxx8e32
' }, // password: password123
];

// JWT Secret Key (should be stored in an environment variable)
const SECRET_KEY = 'yourSecretKey';

// Login route
router.post('/login', async (req, res) => {
  const { username, password } = req.body;

  // Check if user exists
```

```
const user = users.find(u => u.username === username);
if (!user) {
  return res.status(404).json({ message: 'User not found' });
}

// Verify the password
const isMatch = await bcrypt.compare(password, user.password);
if (!isMatch) {
  return res.status(400).json({ message: 'Invalid credentials' });
}

// Create a JWT token
const token = jwt.sign({ id: user.id, username: user.username },
SECRET_KEY, { expiresIn: '1h' });

// Respond with the token
res.json({ token });
});

module.exports = router;
```

In this example:

- The password is **hashed** with **bcryptjs** before being stored, and when the user logs in, the entered password is compared against the hashed password.
- If the credentials are valid, a **JWT token** is generated and sent back to the client.

- The token contains user information (ID and username), and it is signed with a secret key. The token expires in 1 hour (expiresIn: '1h').

---

3. Protecting Routes with JWT-Based Authentication

Once the user has a JWT token, they can include it in the Authorization header of their requests to protected routes. You'll need to protect certain routes, ensuring that only authenticated users with a valid JWT token can access them.

Here's how you can protect a route using the authenticateToken middleware we defined earlier:

Step 1: Protecting Routes

Now, let's create a protected route in userRoute.js that only authenticated users can access:

js

```js
const express = require('express');
const { authenticateToken } = require('./authMiddleware'); // Import the authentication middleware
const router = express.Router();

// Protected route
router.get('/profile', authenticateToken, (req, res) => {
```

```
res.json({
  message: 'This is a protected route',
  user: req.user, // The user data attached from the token
  });
});
```

```
module.exports = router;
```

In this example:

- The profile route is protected using the authenticateToken middleware.
- If the request includes a valid JWT token, the middleware will allow the request to proceed and return the user's profile.
- If the token is missing, invalid, or expired, the request will be denied with an appropriate error message.

---

4. Testing JWT Authentication with Postman

Now that we've set up JWT authentication, it's important to test it to ensure everything works as expected. **Postman** is a great tool for testing API endpoints.

Step 1: Testing the Login Endpoint

1. Open Postman.
2. Set the request method to **POST**.

3. Enter the URL for the login route (e.g., http://localhost:3000/login).

4. In the body of the request, select **raw** and set the format to **JSON**. Add the credentials:

json

```
{
  "username": "user1",
  "password": "password123"
}
```

5. Send the request. If successful, the server will respond with a JWT token.

Step 2: Testing the Protected Endpoint

1. Open a new request tab in Postman.

2. Set the request method to **GET**.

3. Enter the URL for the protected route (e.g., http://localhost:3000/profile).

4. In the **Authorization** tab, select **Bearer Token** and paste the JWT token obtained from the login response.

5. Send the request. If the token is valid, the server will return the protected data.

In this chapter, we've covered the essentials of **JWT authentication** in **Node.js**. You learned how to:

- Set up JWT authentication in your Node.js application.
- Create a simple login system that issues JWT tokens.
- Protect routes using JWT-based authentication.

JWT provides a powerful and flexible way to handle authentication in modern web applications. With this knowledge, you can build secure APIs that allow users to log in and access protected resources using stateless tokens.

Chapter 15: Securing Your API

Securing an API is essential to protect sensitive data and ensure that only authorized users can access specific endpoints. In this chapter, we will explore techniques to protect your API from common security threats. We will cover encrypting sensitive data, securing API endpoints with HTTPS, and implementing rate-limiting and IP blocking to prevent abuse.

1. Protecting Sensitive Data with Encryption

Sensitive data, such as passwords, personal information, and API keys, should never be stored or transmitted in plaintext. Encryption ensures that even if data is intercepted, it cannot be read by unauthorized parties.

Step 1: Password Hashing

Passwords are one of the most sensitive pieces of data that you need to protect. Storing passwords as plain text is a major security risk. Instead, you should **hash** passwords before storing them. **Hashing** is a one-way encryption process that transforms the password into a fixed-length string. This string cannot be reversed to retrieve the original password.

To hash passwords securely in Node.js, you can use the **bcryptjs** library. Here's how you can hash and compare passwords:

1. **Hashing a password** when the user signs up:

js

```
const bcrypt = require('bcryptjs');

// Hashing the password before saving it to the database
const salt = bcrypt.genSaltSync(10); // Number of rounds for salting
const hashedPassword = bcrypt.hashSync(userPassword, salt);

// Save hashedPassword to the database
```

2. **Verifying the password** when the user logs in:

js

```
const isPasswordCorrect = bcrypt.compareSync(userInputPassword, storedHashedPassword);

if (isPasswordCorrect) {
  // Allow login
} else {
  // Reject login attempt
}
```

Step 2: Encrypting Sensitive Data

Sometimes, you may need to encrypt sensitive data beyond passwords, such as API keys or credit card information. You can use the **crypto** module in Node.js to perform encryption and decryption.

Example of encrypting data:

js

```js
const crypto = require('crypto');

// Secret key for encryption (store this securely)
const secretKey = 'yourSecretKey';

// Encrypting data
const encryptData = (data) => {
  const cipher = crypto.createCipher('aes-256-ctr', secretKey);
  let encrypted = cipher.update(data, 'utf8', 'hex');
  encrypted += cipher.final('hex');
  return encrypted;
};

// Decrypting data
const decryptData = (encryptedData) => {
  const decipher = crypto.createDecipher('aes-256-ctr', secretKey);
  let decrypted = decipher.update(encryptedData, 'hex', 'utf8');
  decrypted += decipher.final('utf8');
  return decrypted;
};
```

```
// Example usage
const sensitiveData = 'API_SECRET_KEY';
const encryptedData = encryptData(sensitiveData);
const decryptedData = decryptData(encryptedData);
```

Using encryption in combination with hashing ensures that even if your data is intercepted, it remains secure.

---

2. Securing API Endpoints with HTTPS

HTTP requests sent over the internet are vulnerable to being intercepted by attackers, especially if they contain sensitive information. This is where **HTTPS (Hypertext Transfer Protocol Secure)** comes into play. HTTPS encrypts the data transmitted between the client and the server, making it much more difficult for attackers to intercept and read the data.

Step 1: Setting Up HTTPS on Your Node.js Server

To enable HTTPS on your Node.js server, you'll need an SSL/TLS certificate. You can obtain a certificate from a Certificate Authority (CA) or use a self-signed certificate for development purposes.

1. **Generate a self-signed certificate (for local development)**: You can use **OpenSSL** to generate a self-signed certificate:

bash

```
openssl genrsa -out privatekey.pem 2048
openssl req -new -key privatekey.pem -out cert.csr
openssl x509 -req -days 365 -in cert.csr -signkey privatekey.pem -out certificate.pem
```

2. **Set up HTTPS in your Node.js server**: Modify your server.js (or equivalent) file to use HTTPS:

js

```js
const fs = require('fs');
const https = require('https');
const express = require('express');
const app = express();

// Load SSL certificate and private key
const privateKey = fs.readFileSync('privatekey.pem', 'utf8');
const certificate = fs.readFileSync('certificate.pem', 'utf8');
const credentials = { key: privateKey, cert: certificate };

// Set up HTTPS server
https.createServer(credentials, app).listen(3000, () => {
  console.log('Server running on https://localhost:3000');
});

// Example route
app.get('/', (req, res) => {
  res.send('Secure API');
```

```
});
```

Step 2: Forcing HTTPS Redirect

While using HTTPS ensures encryption, users may still try to access your API over HTTP. To enforce the use of HTTPS, you can redirect all HTTP traffic to HTTPS:

js

```js
const express = require('express');
const app = express();

// Redirect HTTP requests to HTTPS
app.use((req, res, next) => {
  if (req.protocol !== 'https') {
    return res.redirect(301, `https://${req.headers.host}${req.url}`);
  }
  next();
});
```

```
// Other routes and server setup...
```

Now, when users try to access your API using HTTP, they will be automatically redirected to HTTPS.

---

3. Implementing Rate-Limiting and IP Blocking to Prevent Abuse

APIs can become vulnerable to abuse if they are not protected against excessive or malicious requests. Two common methods for securing your API from abuse are **rate-limiting** and **IP blocking**.

Step 1: Rate-Limiting

Rate-limiting restricts the number of requests that can be made to your API within a specified time window. It helps prevent brute-force attacks and ensures fair usage of the API.

You can use the **express-rate-limit** package to implement rate-limiting in your Express API.

1. **Install the package**:

bash

```
npm install express-rate-limit
```

2. **Set up rate-limiting** in your API:

js

```
const rateLimit = require('express-rate-limit');

// Create a rate-limiting rule
const limiter = rateLimit({
  windowMs: 15 * 60 * 1000, // 15 minutes
  max: 100, // limit each IP to 100 requests per window
  message: 'Too many requests from this IP, please try again later.'
});
```

```
// Apply the rate-limiting rule to all routes
app.use(limiter);
```

In this example, each IP address is allowed a maximum of 100 requests within a 15-minute window. If an IP exceeds this limit, they will receive an error message and be blocked temporarily.

Step 2: IP Blocking

IP blocking allows you to block requests from specific IP addresses. This is especially useful if an IP address is known to be malicious or if you want to restrict access to certain users.

You can manually block IPs by checking the IP address in your middleware:

js

```
const blockedIPs = ['192.168.1.100', '203.0.113.5']; // Example list of blocked IPs

app.use((req, res, next) => {
  if (blockedIPs.includes(req.ip)) {
    return res.status(403).json({ message: 'Access denied from this IP' });
  }
  next();
});
```

In this example, the API checks the incoming request's IP address (req.ip) and compares it against a list of blocked IPs. If the IP is found in the list, the request is rejected.

You can also use third-party services like **Cloudflare** or **AWS WAF** to handle IP blocking and other advanced security features.

Securing your API is not optional; it's a critical step in protecting your data, users, and overall system integrity. By using encryption for sensitive data, enforcing HTTPS to protect communication, and implementing rate-limiting and IP blocking to prevent abuse, you can ensure that your API is both functional and secure.

As you build APIs, remember that security is an ongoing process. Stay up-to-date with security best practices and continuously monitor your system to address any potential vulnerabilities.

Chapter 16: Role-Based Access Control (RBAC)

Role-Based Access Control (RBAC) is a method for restricting system access to authorized users based on their roles within an organization or system. Implementing RBAC ensures that users can only access resources that are necessary for their role, helping protect sensitive data and functionality. In this chapter, we will explain what RBAC is, why it is important, and how to implement it in your API. We will also cover protecting routes based on user roles (e.g., admin vs. regular user).

1. What is RBAC and Why is It Important?

RBAC is a widely used access control mechanism in software systems. It is based on the concept of **roles** and **permissions**. Each role has a specific set of permissions that determine what actions the user can perform. These permissions are assigned to users according to their job functions.

For example:

- **Admin**: Can create, read, update, and delete resources.
- **User**: Can only read and create resources.
- **Guest**: Can only view public information.

Importance of RBAC

RBAC is critical for several reasons:

- **Security**: By limiting user access to only the resources they need, RBAC minimizes the risk of unauthorized access and data breaches.
- **Scalability**: Managing roles and permissions is easier than assigning individual permissions to each user, especially as the number of users grows.
- **Compliance**: Many organizations must follow regulatory requirements to ensure that sensitive data is protected. RBAC helps implement these security measures effectively.
- **Ease of Maintenance**: By grouping permissions into roles, it becomes easier to maintain and update access rights. If a role needs additional permissions, they can be added to the role rather than being managed per user.

---

2. Implementing Role-Based Permissions in Your API

To implement RBAC in your API, you first need to define the roles and permissions. Then, you need to create a mechanism to check the user's role before allowing them to access certain routes.

Step 1: Defining Roles and Permissions

In a typical RBAC system, roles are assigned to users, and each role has a specific set of permissions. You can define roles as follows:

js

```
const roles = {
  ADMIN: 'admin',
  USER: 'user',
  GUEST: 'guest'
};

const permissions = {
  CREATE: 'create',
  READ: 'read',
  UPDATE: 'update',
  DELETE: 'delete'
};
```

For example, an **admin** can perform all actions, while a **user** can only read and create resources.

Step 2: Assigning Roles to Users

When a user registers or logs in, they should be assigned a role. This role will typically be stored in the database along with other user information.

Here's how you might define a user model with a role:

js

```
const mongoose = require('mongoose');
const Schema = mongoose.Schema;

const userSchema = new Schema({
  username: { type: String, required: true },
  password: { type: String, required: true },
  role: { type: String, enum: [roles.ADMIN, roles.USER, roles.GUEST], default:
roles.USER }
});

const User = mongoose.model('User', userSchema);

module.exports = User;
```

In this example, the user has a role field that can be set to either admin, user, or guest.

Step 3: Checking User Role Before Granting Access

Now that the roles and permissions are defined, you can create middleware to check if the logged-in user has the necessary role to access a specific route. This middleware will verify the user's role based on the JWT token or session data.

Here's an example middleware to protect routes based on user roles:

js

```
const jwt = require('jsonwebtoken');

// Role-based access control middleware
```

```
const roleAuthorization = (requiredRole) => {
  return (req, res, next) => {
    // Get the JWT token from headers (or cookies)
    const token = req.headers['authorization']?.split(' ')[1];

    if (!token) {
      return res.status(403).json({ message: 'No token provided' });
    }

    try {
      // Verify the JWT token
      const decoded = jwt.verify(token, 'yourSecretKey');
      req.user = decoded; // Attach decoded user data to the request object

      // Check if user role matches the required role
      if (req.user.role !== requiredRole) {
        return res.status(403).json({ message: 'Forbidden: Insufficient role' });
      }

      // User has the correct role, proceed to the next middleware
      next();
    } catch (error) {
      return res.status(401).json({ message: 'Unauthorized: Invalid token' });
    }
  };
};

module.exports = roleAuthorization;
```

Step 4: Protecting Routes Based on Roles

Once the middleware is created, you can use it to protect specific routes. For instance, only an **admin** should have access to the /admin route:

js

```js
const express = require('express');
const router = express.Router();
const roleAuthorization = require('./middlewares/roleAuthorization');

// Admin route, accessible only by admins
router.get('/admin', roleAuthorization(roles.ADMIN), (req, res) => {
  res.status(200).json({ message: 'Welcome Admin' });
});

// User route, accessible by users and admins
router.get('/user', roleAuthorization(roles.USER), (req, res) => {
  res.status(200).json({ message: 'Welcome User' });
});

module.exports = router;
```

In this example:

- The /admin route is protected by the roleAuthorization middleware, and only users with the admin role can access it.
- The /user route is protected, but it can be accessed by both **users** and **admins**.

Step 5: Handling Multiple Roles with Permissions

Sometimes, you may need more granular control over user permissions. For example, an **admin** can perform all actions, but a **user** might be able to create or read resources but not delete them.

To implement this:

1. Define a **permissions** model.
2. Assign specific permissions to roles.

Here's an example of how to set this up:

js

```js
const permissions = {
  CREATE: 'create',
  READ: 'read',
  UPDATE: 'update',
  DELETE: 'delete'
};
```

```js
// Define permissions for each role
const rolePermissions = {
  [roles.ADMIN]: [permissions.CREATE, permissions.READ,
permissions.UPDATE, permissions.DELETE],
  [roles.USER]: [permissions.READ, permissions.CREATE],
  [roles.GUEST]: [permissions.READ]
};
```

```js
// Middleware to check if the user has specific permission
const permissionAuthorization = (requiredPermission) => {
```

```
return (req, res, next) => {
  const token = req.headers['authorization']?.split(' ')[1];

  if (!token) {
    return res.status(403).json({ message: 'No token provided' });
  }

  try {
    const decoded = jwt.verify(token, 'yourSecretKey');
    req.user = decoded;

    const userPermissions = rolePermissions[req.user.role] || [];

    if (!userPermissions.includes(requiredPermission)) {
      return res.status(403).json({ message: 'Forbidden: Insufficient permission'
});
    }

    next();
  } catch (error) {
    return res.status(401).json({ message: 'Unauthorized: Invalid token' });
  }
};
};
```

Now you can use the permissionAuthorization middleware to protect routes with specific permissions:

js

```
router.post('/create-resource',   permissionAuthorization(permissions.CREATE),
(req, res) => {
 res.status(200).json({ message: 'Resource created' });
});


router.delete('/delete-resource', permissionAuthorization(permissions.DELETE),
(req, res) => {
 res.status(200).json({ message: 'Resource deleted' });
});
```

3. Best Practices for Implementing RBAC

- **Minimal Privilege**: Always give users the minimal set of permissions they need to perform their job functions. This reduces the risk of unauthorized access.

- **Role Granularity**: Use multiple roles with varying levels of permissions rather than just "admin" or "user" roles. This provides more flexibility and security.

- **Auditing and Monitoring**: Regularly audit access control logs to track who is accessing your system and verify that they have the appropriate permissions.

- **Keep Role Data Secure**: Ensure that role and permission data is stored securely and encrypted if needed, especially when dealing with sensitive information.

Role-Based Access Control is an essential part of securing your API, ensuring that users can only access resources based on their roles and permissions. By defining roles, assigning permissions, and protecting routes accordingly, you can ensure a secure, scalable, and maintainable API system. RBAC is a critical piece of security best practices that helps prevent unauthorized access to sensitive data and protects your application from misuse.

Chapter 17: Building File Upload and Download APIs

In this chapter, we will explore how to build file upload and download functionality into your API. File handling is an essential feature in many applications, whether it's for managing user-generated content, storing documents, or processing images. By the end of this chapter, you will have the knowledge to implement file upload and download capabilities using Node.js, along with practical guidance on storing files locally or on cloud services like AWS S3 and Google Cloud Storage.

---

1. Handling File Uploads in Node.js (Using Multer)

Node.js, being a backend platform, can handle file uploads with the help of middleware. **Multer** is a popular middleware for handling multipart/form-data, which is used for uploading files. Multer processes the incoming file data, stores the file in a specified location, and adds metadata to the request object.

Installing Multer

To start handling file uploads in your Node.js API, you'll need to install the **Multer** package. Run the following command to install it:

bash

npm install multer

Basic File Upload Setup

Here's how to set up a basic file upload functionality using Multer in an Express app:

js

```js
const express = require('express');
const multer = require('multer');
const path = require('path');
const app = express();

// Set up storage options (destination and filename)
const storage = multer.diskStorage({
  destination: (req, file, cb) => {
    cb(null, './uploads');  // Directory where files will be saved
  },
  filename: (req, file, cb) => {
    cb(null, Date.now() + path.extname(file.originalname)); // Unique filename
  }
});

// Initialize multer with storage settings
const upload = multer({ storage: storage });

// Set up a route to handle file upload
app.post('/upload', upload.single('file'), (req, res) => {
  if (!req.file) {
```

```
  return res.status(400).json({ message: 'No file uploaded' });
}
res.status(200).json({
  message: 'File uploaded successfully',
  file: req.file
});
});

app.listen(3000, () => {
  console.log('Server running on port 3000');
});
```

In the code above:

- We define the storage object to set up the destination directory (uploads/) and the filename for the uploaded file.
- The upload.single('file') middleware is used to handle a single file upload from a form field named file.
- The file metadata (such as originalname, mimetype, and size) is automatically attached to the req.file object.

Handling Multiple File Uploads

To handle multiple file uploads, you can use upload.array() or upload.fields(). For example:

js

```
app.post('/uploadMultiple', upload.array('files', 10), (req, res) => {
  if (!req.files || req.files.length === 0) {
    return res.status(400).json({ message: 'No files uploaded' });
```

```
  }
  res.status(200).json({
    message: 'Files uploaded successfully',
    files: req.files
  });
});
```

This example allows you to upload up to 10 files at once, and each file is accessible via req.files.

---

2. Storing Files Locally or on Cloud Services

Once a file is uploaded, you need to decide where to store it. There are two main options: local storage or cloud storage services like **AWS S3** or **Google Cloud Storage**.

Storing Files Locally

In the previous example, files were saved locally on the server's filesystem in the uploads/ directory. This approach is simple and fast for small applications or development purposes, but it may not scale well for large volumes of files or for distributed systems.

Storing Files on Cloud Services

For production applications, it's often better to use a cloud service to store files, which offers advantages like scalability, security, and redundancy. AWS S3 and Google Cloud Storage are two popular options.

AWS S3 Integration

To upload files to **AWS S3**, you need to install the aws-sdk:

bash

```
npm install aws-sdk multer-s3
```

Then, configure S3 storage with Multer and AWS SDK:

js

```js
const AWS = require('aws-sdk');
const multerS3 = require('multer-s3');

// Configure AWS S3
AWS.config.update({
  accessKeyId: 'your-aws-access-key',
  secretAccessKey: 'your-aws-secret-key',
  region: 'your-region'
});

const s3 = new AWS.S3();

// Set up Multer storage to upload directly to S3
const storage = multerS3({
  s3: s3,
  bucket: 'your-bucket-name',
  acl: 'public-read', // The file will be publicly accessible
  metadata: (req, file, cb) => {
    cb(null, { fieldName: file.fieldname });
  },
  key: (req, file, cb) => {
```

```
  cb(null, `uploads/${Date.now()}-${file.originalname}`);
 }
});


// Create Multer upload instance
const upload = multer({ storage: storage });


// API endpoint for file upload to S3
app.post('/uploadS3', upload.single('file'), (req, res) => {
 if (!req.file) {
  return res.status(400).json({ message: 'No file uploaded' });
 }
 res.status(200).json({
  message: 'File uploaded to S3 successfully',
  file: req.file
 });
});
```

In this code:

- We configure AWS S3 with the appropriate credentials.
- We use multer-s3 to upload the file directly to an S3 bucket.
- The file is uploaded to the uploads/ folder in the specified S3 bucket with a unique filename.

Google Cloud Storage Integration

To store files on **Google Cloud Storage**, you need the @google-cloud/storage package:

bash

npm install @google-cloud/storage multer

Then, set up Google Cloud Storage:

js

```js
const { Storage } = require('@google-cloud/storage');
const multer = require('multer');
const storage = new Storage();

// Create a Multer instance to handle file uploads to Google Cloud Storage
const multerStorage = multer.diskStorage({
  destination: (req, file, cb) => {
    cb(null, './uploads/');
  },
  filename: (req, file, cb) => {
    cb(null, file.originalname);
  }
});

const uploadToCloud = multer({ storage: multerStorage });

app.post('/uploadToCloud', uploadToCloud.single('file'), (req, res) => {
  if (!req.file) {
    return res.status(400).json({ message: 'No file uploaded' });
  }

  const bucket = storage.bucket('your-bucket-name');
  const blob = bucket.file(req.file.filename);
  const blobStream = blob.createWriteStream();

  blobStream.on('finish', () => {
```

```
res.status(200).json({ message: 'File uploaded to Google Cloud Storage
successfully' });
  });

  blobStream.on('error', (err) => {
    res.status(500).json({ message: 'Error uploading file', error: err });
  });

  blobStream.end(req.file.buffer);
});
```

---

3. Creating an API for Downloading Files

Once a file is uploaded, it is often necessary to allow users to download it. You can create a simple endpoint for serving files to users.

Serving Local Files

If the file is stored locally, you can use the express.static middleware to serve it directly to clients:

js

```
app.use('/uploads', express.static('uploads'));
```

This will serve files in the uploads/ directory when the user accesses the /uploads/ path. For example, a file uploaded as uploads/example.txt would be accessible at http://localhost:3000/uploads/example.txt.

Serving Files from Cloud Storage

If the file is stored on a cloud service like AWS S3, you can generate a presigned URL to allow users to securely download the file.

Here's an example for AWS S3:

js

```
app.get('/downloadS3/:filename', (req, res) => {
  const params = {
    Bucket: 'your-bucket-name',
    Key: `uploads/${req.params.filename}`,
    Expires: 60 // URL expires in 60 seconds
  };

  s3.getSignedUrl('getObject', params, (err, url) => {
    if (err) {
      return res.status(500).json({ message: 'Error generating download URL',
error: err });
    }
    res.status(200).json({ downloadUrl: url });
  });
});
```

This route generates a presigned URL that can be used to download the file directly from S3.

Building file upload and download APIs with Node.js is a crucial feature for many modern applications. By using Multer and integrating with cloud storage services such as AWS S3 or Google Cloud Storage, you can easily manage file storage, improve scalability, and ensure the security of your files. With the ability to serve files locally or through presigned URLs from cloud services, your API will be ready to handle file-related tasks effectively and securely.

Chapter 18: Working with External APIs

In this chapter, we'll explore how to integrate external APIs into your Node.js application. Often, your application needs to interact with third-party services, such as weather data providers, social media platforms, or payment gateways. By the end of this chapter, you will learn how to make HTTP requests to external APIs, handle the responses, and integrate this data into your own API.

1. Making API Requests to Third-Party Services (e.g., via Axios or node-fetch)

To communicate with external APIs, we need to send HTTP requests. In Node.js, there are several libraries available to make HTTP requests, with **Axios** and **node-fetch** being two of the most popular.

Using Axios

Axios is a promise-based HTTP client that makes it easy to send asynchronous HTTP requests from Node.js. It's particularly useful for working with REST APIs due to its simplicity and ability to handle both GET and POST requests efficiently.

Installing Axios

To install Axios, run the following command:

bash

npm install axios

Making a Simple GET Request with Axios

Here's an example of making a GET request to an external API (e.g., retrieving user data from a JSONPlaceholder API):

js

```
const axios = require('axios');

axios.get('https://jsonplaceholder.typicode.com/users')
  .then(response => {
    console.log(response.data);  // Accessing the response data
  })
  .catch(error => {
    console.error('Error fetching data:', error);
  });
```

In this example:

- We use axios.get() to fetch data from a placeholder API.
- The response data is returned in the .then() block and printed to the console.
- Errors are caught in the .catch() block.

Using node-fetch

Another lightweight alternative to Axios is **node-fetch**, a minimalistic library that implements the window.fetch API for

Node.js. It's a great choice if you prefer a smaller library or are familiar with the fetch API from client-side JavaScript.

Installing node-fetch

To install node-fetch, run:

bash

npm install node-fetch

Making a Simple GET Request with node-fetch

js

```
const fetch = require('node-fetch');

fetch('https://jsonplaceholder.typicode.com/users')
  .then(response => response.json()) // Convert the response to JSON
  .then(data => {
   console.log(data); // Accessing the response data
  })
  .catch(error => {
   console.error('Error fetching data:', error);
  });
```

Here:

- fetch() is used to send the request to the API.
- We convert the response into a JSON object using response.json(), and then access it in the .then() block.
- Any errors during the request are caught in the .catch() block.

2. Integrating Third-Party APIs (Weather Data, Social Media APIs, etc.)

Now, let's see how to integrate some common third-party APIs in a Node.js application. We'll walk through examples of integrating a weather API and a social media API.

Weather API Integration

Imagine you want to build an application that shows weather data based on a user's location. We will use the **OpenWeatherMap API** for this purpose.

Setting up OpenWeatherMap API

1. First, you need to sign up on the OpenWeatherMap website and get an API key (this is free for basic usage).
2. Once you have your API key, you can use Axios or node-fetch to send a request to the OpenWeatherMap API.

Example of Fetching Weather Data

js

```
const axios = require('axios');

// Replace with your OpenWeatherMap API key
const apiKey = 'your-api-key';
```

```
const city = 'London';

axios.get(`http://api.openweathermap.org/data/2.5/weather?q=${city}&appid=$
{apiKey}`)
  .then(response => {
    const weatherData = response.data;
    console.log(`The           weather        in          ${city}          is:
${weatherData.weather[0].description}`);
    console.log(`Temperature: ${weatherData.main.temp}°C`);
  })
  .catch(error => {
    console.error('Error fetching weather data:', error);
  });
```

In this example:

- The API request URL is constructed with the city name and API key.

- The response data contains the weather description and temperature, which are logged to the console.

Social Media API Integration (e.g., Twitter)

Many applications require integration with social media platforms. In this example, we will fetch recent tweets using the **Twitter API**.

1. To get started, you'll need to create a Twitter Developer account and obtain the necessary API keys (consumer key, consumer secret, access token, and access token secret).

2. Once you have the keys, you can use libraries such as **Twit** or **twitter-api-v2** to interact with the Twitter API.

Setting up Twit

bash

npm install twit

Fetching Tweets using Twit

js

```
const Twit = require('twit');

// Set up Twitter API credentials
const T = new Twit({
  consumer_key: 'your-consumer-key',
  consumer_secret: 'your-consumer-secret',
  access_token: 'your-access-token',
  access_token_secret: 'your-access-token-secret'
});

// Fetch recent tweets
T.get('statuses/home_timeline', { count: 5 }, (err, data, response) => {
  if (err) {
    console.error('Error fetching tweets:', err);
  } else {
    console.log('Recent Tweets:');
    data.forEach(tweet => {
      console.log(`${tweet.user.name}: ${tweet.text}`);
    });
```

```
 }
});
```

In this example:

- We set up a Twit instance with your Twitter API credentials.
- We use T.get() to request the latest tweets from the authenticated user's timeline.

3. Parsing JSON Responses from External APIs and Using the Data in Your API

When you make API requests to external services, the response is typically in JSON format. You need to parse the response and integrate it into your application.

Parsing JSON Data

Both Axios and node-fetch automatically parse JSON responses, so you can directly access the response data.

js

```
// Axios example
axios.get('https://jsonplaceholder.typicode.com/users')
  .then(response => {
    const users = response.data;
    console.log('Users:', users);  // Accessing the parsed JSON data
  })
```

```
.catch(error => {
  console.error('Error fetching users:', error);
});


// node-fetch example
fetch('https://jsonplaceholder.typicode.com/users')
 .then(response => response.json())
 .then(data => {
  const users = data;
  console.log('Users:', users);  // Accessing the parsed JSON data
 })
 .catch(error => {
  console.error('Error fetching users:', error);
});
```

After parsing the response data, you can use it in your API. For example, you might retrieve weather data or user details from external sources and return them as part of your own API response.

Example: Combining Data from External API with Your API

Let's say we want to create an API that combines weather data with a user profile fetched from an external database. Here's a simple example:

js

```
app.get('/user-profile', (req, res) => {
// Fetch user data from your database
const userProfile = { name: 'John Doe', city: 'London' };
```

```
// Fetch weather data from OpenWeatherMap API

axios.get(`http://api.openweathermap.org/data/2.5/weather?q=${userProfile.city
}&appid=your-api-key`)
  .then(response => {
    const weatherData = response.data;
    userProfile.weather = weatherData.weather[0].description;
    userProfile.temperature = weatherData.main.temp;

    res.json(userProfile);  // Returning combined data
  })
  .catch(error => {
    console.error('Error fetching weather data:', error);
    res.status(500).json({ message: 'Error fetching data' });
  });
});
```

In this example:

- We retrieve the user's profile from a local database (simulated here as an object).
- We fetch the weather data using Axios and merge it with the user profile.
- We return the combined data in the API response.

In this chapter, we covered how to interact with third-party APIs from your Node.js application. You learned how to make requests using **Axios** and **node-fetch**, how to work with different types of external APIs (such as weather and social media), and how to parse JSON responses. We also discussed how to combine external data with your own API responses to create powerful and dynamic applications. With these skills, you can expand the functionality of your APIs and integrate a wide variety of external services to enhance the user experience.

Chapter 19: Versioning Your API

In this chapter, we'll dive into the concept of **API versioning**, a crucial aspect of API development that ensures your application can evolve over time without breaking existing functionality for users. API versioning allows you to introduce new features, make improvements, and fix bugs, all while maintaining compatibility with older versions of your API.

1. Why API Versioning is Important

As your API evolves, new features and changes are introduced that may not be backward-compatible with previous versions. Versioning helps you manage these changes and ensures that consumers of your API can continue using it as expected, without being forced to immediately adopt breaking changes.

Key Reasons for Versioning:

- **Backward Compatibility:** If your API undergoes changes that break existing functionality (e.g., removing fields or altering data formats), versioning ensures that old clients still work with the older version of the API.
- **Grace Period for Migration:** When you release a new version, clients using the older version can continue

working without disruption, giving them time to migrate to the new version at their own pace.

- **Flexibility for New Features:** API versioning allows you to introduce new features and endpoints without worrying about breaking existing functionality.
- **Clear Communication:** It provides a clear way to communicate changes and improvements to consumers of the API, making it easier to manage expectations.

Without versioning, you risk forcing your users to adopt new changes immediately, which can be disruptive and lead to frustration.

2. Strategies for Versioning Your API

There are several strategies for versioning APIs, each with its pros and cons. Let's explore the most common approaches:

1. URI Versioning (Path Versioning)

URI versioning is one of the most popular and straightforward methods. In this approach, the version is included directly in the URL path of the API endpoint. This method is easy to understand, and it's immediately visible when users or developers interact with your API.

Example:

plaintext

https://api.example.com/v1/users

https://api.example.com/v2/users

In this example, the version number (v1, v2) is part of the endpoint URL. When the API evolves, the version number in the URL is updated to reflect the changes.

Pros of URI Versioning:

- **Simple and intuitive:** The version is clearly visible in the URL, making it easy for both developers and consumers to know which version they are working with.

- **No ambiguity:** Each version of the API is treated as a completely separate endpoint, so there's no ambiguity in routing requests.

Cons of URI Versioning:

- **Redundancy in URLs:** You may end up with redundant or long URLs, especially as the API grows and more versions are introduced.

- **Overhead:** As your API evolves, maintaining multiple versions can become cumbersome, requiring you to manage different branches and endpoints.

2. Header Versioning

With header versioning, the version of the API is specified in the request headers rather than the URL. This method allows you to keep your API URLs clean and focused on the functionality, while still providing flexibility for versioning.

Example:

http

```
GET /users
Host: api.example.com
Accept: application/vnd.example.v1+json
```

In this example, the version of the API is specified using the Accept header, and the client sends the version they want (in this case, version 1).

Pros of Header Versioning:

- **Cleaner URLs:** The URL remains free from versioning details, which can make it easier to work with and more aesthetically pleasing.
- **More flexible:** You can specify the version dynamically through headers, allowing for multiple versions to coexist in the same URL structure.

Cons of Header Versioning:

- **Less visibility:** The version is hidden in the request headers, so it might be harder for developers to quickly identify the version they are working with.
- **More complex:** Clients need to know to specify the correct version in the header, which can add complexity to the API usage.

---

3. Query Parameter Versioning

In this method, the API version is specified as a query parameter in the URL. While not as common as URI versioning, this approach can be useful when you need more flexibility without cluttering the URL path.

Example:

plaintext

```
https://api.example.com/users?version=1
https://api.example.com/users?version=2
```

Pros of Query Parameter Versioning:

- **Simple and flexible:** This approach doesn't require changing the URL structure or using headers, making it easy to specify the version.

- **Readable URLs:** The version information is explicitly part of the URL, but not embedded in the main path, which can still keep URLs fairly clean.

Cons of Query Parameter Versioning:

- **Ambiguity:** Using query parameters for versioning might introduce ambiguity for some developers, as the version is part of the query string and not the path.
- **Less clear intent:** Unlike URI versioning, which clearly indicates a different version of the resource, query parameters are generally used for filtering and sorting data, not for versioning.

---

4. Accept Header Versioning (Content Negotiation)

Another approach is to use the Accept header for versioning, where clients specify which version they want to consume by including the version number in the Accept header.

Example:

http

```
GET /users
Accept: application/vnd.example.v1+json
```

This method uses content negotiation to determine the version of the API being requested based on the Accept header in the HTTP request.

Pros of Accept Header Versioning:

- **Clean URLs:** Like header versioning, it keeps the API URLs clean.
- **Flexible:** The versioning is independent of the URL path, allowing the same URL to serve multiple versions.

Cons of Accept Header Versioning:

- **Complexity:** It requires developers to be familiar with content negotiation and might be more difficult to understand for beginners.
- **Not as obvious:** The version is specified in headers, making it less obvious to the end user what version of the API they are interacting with.

---

3. Best Practices for Maintaining Backwards Compatibility

Once you've chosen a versioning strategy, it's essential to keep backwards compatibility in mind, ensuring that existing users' applications continue to function correctly as your API evolves.

1. Maintain Older Versions for a Grace Period

When you release a new version of your API, it's important to maintain support for older versions for a period of time. This allows consumers to gradually migrate to the new version without causing disruption.

2. Deprecate Old Versions with Clear Communication

If you need to phase out an older version, you should clearly communicate the deprecation timeline to API consumers. This can be done via API documentation, email notifications, or a response header indicating that a version is deprecated and will be removed in the future.

3. Use Semantic Versioning (SemVer)

Semantic Versioning is a versioning scheme that indicates whether a new release introduces backward-compatible changes. It uses three numbers: MAJOR.MINOR.PATCH (e.g., 2.3.1).

- **MAJOR:** Increments indicate breaking changes (e.g., a new version that is not backward-compatible).
- **MINOR:** Increments indicate non-breaking changes, such as new features or functionality that don't affect the existing API.
- **PATCH:** Increments indicate small changes, such as bug fixes or minor tweaks.

By adhering to **SemVer**, you make it clear what kind of changes a new version introduces, allowing users to understand the implications of upgrading their integrations.

Versioning your API is an essential practice that helps ensure your API remains reliable, maintainable, and flexible over time. By using one of the versioning strategies discussed in this chapter, you can manage changes to your API while minimizing disruptions to consumers. Remember to follow best practices for backward compatibility and communicate any breaking changes clearly to avoid confusion and frustration among your users.

Chapter 20: Rate Limiting and Caching

In this chapter, we will explore two critical aspects of building a robust and efficient API: **rate limiting** and **caching**. These techniques are essential for improving API performance, ensuring the stability of your application, and providing a better user experience by preventing abuse and optimizing response times.

1. Implementing Rate Limiting to Control Traffic to Your API

Rate limiting is the process of restricting the number of requests a user can make to your API within a specific period. This is essential to protect your API from overloading, abuse, or misuse, and it ensures fair use of resources by all users. Without rate limiting, users or malicious bots could flood your API with requests, leading to performance degradation or even downtime.

Why Use Rate Limiting?

- **Prevent Abuse:** Rate limiting protects your API from misuse by limiting the number of requests a user can make in a given time frame.

- **Ensure Fair Use:** It ensures that all users have equal access to the resources, preventing a single user or bot from monopolizing API traffic.
- **Protect from DoS Attacks:** By limiting the number of requests, you reduce the risk of **Denial of Service (DoS)** or **Distributed Denial of Service (DDoS)** attacks, where excessive requests are sent to overwhelm the system.
- **Improve Performance:** Rate limiting helps in maintaining optimal performance, especially when dealing with large-scale applications.

How to Implement Rate Limiting in Node.js:

One of the simplest ways to implement rate limiting in an Express-based API is by using the popular package express-rate-limit.

1. **Install express-rate-limit:**

bash

npm install express-rate-limit

2. **Setting up Rate Limiting:**

Here's how you can implement a basic rate limiter:

javascript

```
const express = require('express');
```

```
const rateLimit = require('express-rate-limit');

const app = express();

// Set up rate limiting for all routes
const limiter = rateLimit({
  windowMs: 15 * 60 * 1000, // 15 minutes window
  max: 100, // limit each IP to 100 requests per windowMs
  message: 'Too many requests from this IP, please try again later.',
  standardHeaders: true, // Return rate limit info in the `RateLimit-*` headers
  legacyHeaders: false, // Disable the `X-RateLimit-*` headers
});

// Apply rate limiter to all routes
app.use(limiter);

app.get('/', (req, res) => {
  res.send('Hello, world!');
});

app.listen(3000, () => {
  console.log('Server is running on port 3000');
});
```

In the above example, we are limiting users to **100 requests per 15 minutes**. After exceeding the limit, users will receive a message stating that they've exceeded the allowed number of requests.

2. Using express-rate-limit to Throttle Requests

Throttling requests means controlling the flow of requests, making sure that an API doesn't get overwhelmed by too many requests in a short period. **express-rate-limit** is a simple and effective tool to manage request rates.

Throttle Based on Different Parameters:

- **IP Address:** The most common approach to throttling is to limit the requests from a particular IP address.
- **API Key/Authentication Token:** Rate limiting can also be applied based on an API key or authentication token. This is useful when different users have different access levels.

For example, you can customize the rate limiter to track the number of requests based on an API key:

javascript

```javascript
const rateLimit = require('express-rate-limit');

const limiter = rateLimit({
  keyGenerator: (req) => req.headers['x-api-key'], // Use API key for rate limiting
  windowMs: 60 * 1000, // 1 minute window
  max: 5, // 5 requests per minute per API key
  message: 'API key rate limit exceeded, please try again later.'
});
```

This setup ensures that different users, identified by their API keys, are rate-limited independently.

3. Implementing Caching with Redis to Improve Performance

Caching is an essential technique for improving the performance and scalability of your API. It involves storing the results of expensive operations (like database queries or API calls) in a temporary storage layer (the cache) so that future requests can access the cached data quickly without performing the same expensive operations repeatedly.

Why Use Caching?

- **Reduce Latency:** By caching the results of frequent queries, you can return data much faster than querying a database or performing computations every time.
- **Reduce Server Load:** Caching offloads your database and backend services by reducing the need to repeatedly access the same data.
- **Improve Scalability:** Efficient caching allows your API to handle more requests by reducing the time spent on repetitive operations.

Setting Up Redis for Caching:

Redis is a popular in-memory data store that is commonly used for caching in APIs. Redis is fast, scalable, and easy to integrate with Node.js.

1. Install Redis and Redis Client:

You need to have Redis installed on your machine or use a cloud-based Redis service like Redis Labs. You will also need the redis package for your Node.js application:

bash

```
npm install redis
```

2. Set Up a Redis Client in Node.js:

javascript

```
const redis = require('redis');
const express = require('express');

const app = express();
const client = redis.createClient(); // Connect to the local Redis instance

client.on('error', (err) => {
  console.log('Error ' + err);
});

// Set up a basic route
app.get('/data', (req, res) => {
```

```
const key = 'someDataKey';

// Try to fetch data from Redis cache
client.get(key, (err, cachedData) => {
  if (cachedData) {
    // If data is cached, return it
    return res.json(JSON.parse(cachedData));
  }

  // Simulate fetching data from a database or expensive operation
  const data = { message: 'Fetched from the DB or expensive API call.' };

  // Cache the result in Redis with an expiration time (e.g., 60 seconds)
  client.setex(key, 60, JSON.stringify(data));

  // Return the newly fetched data
  res.json(data);
  });
});

app.listen(3000, () => {
  console.log('Server is running on port 3000');
});
```

In the above example:

- The API first checks if the data is already available in Redis.
- If the data exists in the cache, it is returned immediately (reducing latency).

- If the data is not found in the cache, the server fetches it (from a database or external API), stores it in Redis, and sends the response to the client.

- The cached data expires after 60 seconds (client.setex), ensuring that it is not stale.

In this chapter, we've covered two critical techniques for building efficient and scalable APIs: **rate limiting** and **caching**.

- **Rate limiting** ensures that your API can handle traffic effectively and prevents abuse, while also offering fair usage for all users.

- **Caching** with tools like Redis allows you to dramatically improve the performance and scalability of your API by reducing the load on backend systems and speeding up response times.

By implementing these techniques, you can optimize your API for real-world use, offering better user experiences and more reliable service.

Chapter 21: Testing Your API

In this chapter, we will dive into the importance of **testing** in API development and provide practical guidance on how to test your Node.js APIs to ensure reliability and robustness. Testing is a vital step in the development process, as it helps identify and fix bugs, ensures your API behaves as expected, and provides confidence when deploying your API into production.

1. Why Testing Is Essential for API Development

APIs are the backbone of modern web applications, and just like any software, they need to be thoroughly tested to ensure they perform as expected. Here are the key reasons why testing your API is essential:

Reliability:
Testing helps ensure that your API performs consistently under different scenarios, reducing the chances of bugs in production and providing reliability to your users.

Security:
By testing authentication and authorization flows, you can identify and patch potential vulnerabilities before they are exploited. API

security testing is critical to prevent unauthorized access and data breaches.

Performance:

API performance can directly impact the user experience, so testing helps identify performance bottlenecks such as slow endpoints or inefficient database queries.

Regression Testing:

As your API evolves, new features or changes might unintentionally break existing functionality. Regression testing ensures that new changes don't break existing routes or endpoints.

Faster Debugging:

With proper tests in place, debugging becomes easier and faster. Instead of manually testing each part of the application, you can run automated tests to quickly identify where things went wrong.

Confidence:

Testing ensures that you are confident in the API's stability, reducing the likelihood of issues post-deployment.

---

2. Writing Unit Tests for API Routes Using Mocha and Chai

Mocha:

Mocha is a feature-rich JavaScript test framework that runs on Node.js and in the browser, making it ideal for testing API routes. It provides a flexible and easy-to-use API for writing tests.

Chai:

Chai is an assertion library that pairs well with Mocha. It allows you to assert conditions in your tests using a readable and expressive syntax. Chai supports several styles of assertions: should, expect, and assert.

Let's walk through the steps of setting up Mocha and Chai for testing your API.

1. **Install Mocha, Chai, and Supertest (for HTTP assertions):**

bash

```
npm install mocha chai supertest --save-dev
```

2. **Setting Up a Basic Test File:**

Create a test directory in your project root and add a test file (e.g., api.test.js).

javascript

```
const request = require('supertest');
const chai = require('chai');
```

```
const expect = chai.expect;
const app = require('../app'); // Your Express app

describe('GET /users', function() {
  it('should return a list of users', function(done) {
    request(app)
      .get('/users')
      .end(function(err, res) {
        if (err) return done(err);

        // Assert that the response status code is 200
        expect(res.status).to.equal(200);

        // Assert that the response body is an array
        expect(res.body).to.be.an('array');

        done();
      });
  });
});
```

In this example:

- **supertest** is used to make HTTP requests to your API.
- **chai** is used for assertions.
- **request(app)** makes a GET request to the /users route of the Express app, and then we check that the status code is 200 and the response body is an array.

3. **Running the Tests:**

To run the tests, add a script in your package.json:

json

```
"scripts": {
  "test": "mocha"
}
```

Then run:

bash

npm test

This will execute the test and output the results in the terminal.

---

3. Testing Authentication and Authorization

API authentication and authorization are critical security features that require careful testing to ensure that only authorized users can access protected endpoints.

Testing Authentication:

For testing authentication, you should check whether valid credentials grant access and invalid credentials are properly rejected.

Here is an example using JWT authentication:

1. **Testing JWT Authentication:**

javascript

```
describe('POST /login', function() {
  it('should return a JWT token for valid credentials', function(done) {
    const user = { username: 'testuser', password: 'testpassword' };

    request(app)
      .post('/login')
      .send(user)
      .end(function(err, res) {
        if (err) return done(err);

        expect(res.status).to.equal(200);
        expect(res.body.token).to.be.a('string');

        done();
      });
  });
});

  it('should return an error for invalid credentials', function(done) {
    const user = { username: 'wronguser', password: 'wrongpassword' };

    request(app)
      .post('/login')
      .send(user)
      .end(function(err, res) {
        if (err) return done(err);

        expect(res.status).to.equal(401);
        expect(res.body.message).to.equal('Authentication failed');
```

```
    done();
  });
 });
});
```

In the first test, we send valid login credentials and assert that a token is returned. In the second test, we check for the response when invalid credentials are used.

Testing Authorization:

For testing authorization, you should verify that only users with the proper permissions or roles can access protected routes.

javascript

```
describe('GET /admin', function() {
  it('should allow access to an admin user', function(done) {
    const token = 'valid-jwt-token'; // Replace with a valid JWT

    request(app)
      .get('/admin')
      .set('Authorization', `Bearer ${token}`)
      .end(function(err, res) {
        if (err) return done(err);

        expect(res.status).to.equal(200);
        expect(res.body.message).to.equal('Welcome, Admin');

        done();
      });
```

BUILDING APIs WITH NODE.JS

```
});

it('should deny access to a non-admin user', function(done) {
  const token = 'valid-jwt-token-for-user'; // Replace with a non-admin JWT

  request(app)
    .get('/admin')
    .set('Authorization', `Bearer ${token}`)
    .end(function(err, res) {
      if (err) return done(err);

      expect(res.status).to.equal(403);
      expect(res.body.message).to.equal('Access denied');

      done();
    });
  });
});
```

In this example, we test two cases: one where an **admin user** can access the /admin route, and another where a **non-admin user** is denied access.

API testing is an essential step in ensuring the functionality, security, and performance of your application. By using testing frameworks such as **Mocha**, **Chai**, and **Supertest**, you can easily test your API routes, authentication mechanisms, and error handling. This chapter provided practical examples of how to write unit tests, including testing authentication and authorization flows.

With a solid understanding of how to test your API, you can proceed with confidence, knowing that your API is both functional and secure. As we move forward in this book, we will continue to explore other critical aspects of API development, including documentation, deployment, and performance optimization.

Chapter 22: Documenting Your API with Swagger

In this chapter, we will explore the importance of **API documentation** and how to use **Swagger** to automatically generate and maintain comprehensive, interactive, and user-friendly API documentation for your Node.js APIs. Good documentation is essential for both development and collaboration, as it helps other developers understand how to use your API, reduces the learning curve, and ensures consistency in how your API is accessed.

---

1. What is Swagger and How Does It Help with API Documentation?

Swagger (now known as **OpenAPI Specification**) is a powerful set of tools that makes it easier to create, document, and consume RESTful web services. It provides a standardized way to describe your API endpoints, parameters, request/response formats, and authentication methods in a human-readable and machine-readable format.

Swagger allows developers to interact with the API documentation in a way that is almost like using the API itself. It is one of the most widely adopted tools for API documentation due to its simplicity and ease of integration.

Some key features of Swagger:

- **Interactive Documentation:** Swagger generates interactive API documentation that allows developers to test API endpoints directly from the documentation itself.
- **Standardization:** The Swagger specification provides a standardized format for documenting APIs that is easy to read and consistent across projects.
- **Automation:** Swagger can automatically generate and update documentation from your code, reducing the manual work involved in keeping API documentation up-to-date.
- **Integration:** Swagger can be integrated into various frameworks and languages, including Node.js, providing a flexible and cross-platform solution for API documentation.

2. Automatically Generating API Documentation with Swagger UI

Swagger provides an intuitive way to document your API by using the **Swagger UI** tool. This tool generates an interactive web-based UI that displays all the endpoints of your API, their parameters, response formats, and status codes.

Setting Up Swagger in Your Node.js API

To integrate Swagger into your Node.js API, you'll need a few packages:

1. Install the Required Packages:

bash

npm install swagger-ui-express yamljs --save

- **swagger-ui-express** is a middleware for serving Swagger UI in your Express application.
- **yamljs** allows you to load and parse Swagger YAML files into JavaScript objects.

2. Create a Swagger Configuration File:

Create a new file, swagger.yaml, in the root of your project. This YAML file will contain the definition of your API's endpoints, parameters, responses, and metadata.

yaml

```
openapi: 3.0.0
info:
  title: Example API
  description: A simple API for demonstrating Swagger documentation.
  version: 1.0.0
paths:
```

```
/users:
  get:
    summary: Retrieve all users
    responses:
      '200':
        description: A list of users
        content:
          application/json:
            schema:
              type: array
              items:
                type: object
                properties:
                  id:
                    type: integer
                  name:
                    type: string
      '500':
        description: Internal Server Error
```

In this file:

- The info section includes metadata about the API, such as the title, description, and version.
- The paths section defines the available endpoints (e.g., /users) and the HTTP methods (GET, POST, etc.) supported by each endpoint. For the /users endpoint, we define a GET method that retrieves a list of users.

3. **Set Up Swagger UI Middleware in Your Express App:**

Now, integrate Swagger UI into your Express application by adding the following code in your app.js or server.js file:

javascript

```javascript
const express = require('express');
const swaggerUi = require('swagger-ui-express');
const YAML = require('yamljs');

const app = express();
const swaggerDocument = YAML.load('./swagger.yaml');

app.use('/api-docs', swaggerUi.serve, swaggerUi.setup(swaggerDocument));

app.listen(3000, () => {
  console.log('Server is running on http://localhost:3000');
});
```

In this setup:

- **swagger-ui-express.serve** serves the Swagger UI static assets.
- **swagger-ui-express.setup(swaggerDocument)** renders the Swagger UI with the documentation generated from the swagger.yaml file.

Now, when you visit http://localhost:3000/api-docs, you will see the Swagger UI displaying the interactive documentation for your API.

3. Writing Clear and Detailed API Documentation for Developers

While Swagger automates much of the API documentation process, it's essential to ensure the documentation is clear, consistent, and comprehensive for developers who will use your API. Here are some best practices for writing detailed API documentation:

a. Be Descriptive with Endpoint Descriptions

Each API endpoint should have a clear and concise description that explains its functionality. Use the summary and description fields in Swagger to describe what the endpoint does, why it exists, and how it should be used.

Example:

yaml

```
paths:
 /users:
  get:
   summary: Retrieve all users
   description: Fetches a list of all users in the system. This endpoint is useful
for displaying user information in a dashboard.
```

b. Document All Parameters and Request Bodies

For each endpoint, ensure that you document all possible query parameters, URL parameters, and request body properties. Specify their data types, whether they are required or optional, and any constraints (e.g., string length, valid values).

Example:

yaml

```
parameters:
  - name: limit
    in: query
    description: The number of users to return per page
    required: false
    schema:
      type: integer
      default: 10
  - name: name
    in: query
    description: The name of the user to search for
    required: false
    schema:
      type: string
```

c. Provide Clear Response Details

Document the possible responses for each endpoint, including success and error responses. Include the status code, a description of the response, and a schema of the response body.

Example:

yaml

```yaml
responses:
 '200':
   description: A list of users
   content:
    application/json:
     schema:
      type: array
      items:
       type: object
       properties:
        id:
         type: integer
        name:
         type: string
 '400':
   description: Invalid request
 '404':
   description: Users not found
```

d. Include Authentication and Authorization Details

If your API requires authentication (e.g., using JWT), be sure to document the authentication mechanism. Explain how users can authenticate, what tokens are required, and how to send them with API requests.

Example:

yaml

components:

```yaml
securitySchemes:
  BearerAuth:
    type: http
    scheme: bearer
    bearerFormat: JWT


security:
  - BearerAuth: []
```

e. Use Examples for Clarity

Provide example requests and responses to make it easier for developers to understand how to use your API.

Example:

yaml

```yaml
requestBody:
  content:
    application/json:
      example:
        {
          "name": "John Doe",
          "email": "john@example.com"
        }
```

f. Version Your Documentation

As your API evolves, it's important to version your documentation to ensure developers can clearly see changes between versions.

Use the version field in the info section of your Swagger file to track different versions of the API.

Example:

yaml

```
info:
  title: Example API
  description: A simple API for demonstrating Swagger documentation.
  version: 2.0.0
```

In this chapter, we explored how to use Swagger to create clear, interactive, and self-updating documentation for your Node.js API. We learned how to set up Swagger UI, write effective API documentation, and incorporate important features such as authentication, parameters, and response examples. Well-documented APIs improve collaboration and help other developers quickly understand how to interact with your API, ultimately leading to more successful API integrations and smoother development workflows.

Chapter 23: Deploying Your Node.js API

In this chapter, we will cover the steps involved in preparing and deploying your Node.js API to production. Deployment is the final step in the development process, where your API becomes accessible to real users. Proper deployment ensures that your API performs well, remains secure, and can scale to handle increased traffic. We'll also look at automating deployment with CI/CD pipelines, which streamline the process of deploying and updating your API.

---

1. Preparing Your API for Deployment

Before deploying your Node.js API, it's important to ensure that the application is ready for a production environment. This involves several steps to configure environment variables, optimize the application for performance, and ensure it is secure and reliable.

a. Configuring Environment Variables

Environment variables are critical for separating sensitive data (such as API keys, database connection strings, and configuration options) from your source code. In a production environment, it's essential to keep this information secure.

1. **Using .env Files:** The .env file is commonly used to store environment variables locally. In production, these variables should be configured securely on the server or in your cloud provider's dashboard.

   Example .env file:

   makefile

   ```
   DB_HOST=your-database-host
   DB_USER=your-database-user
   DB_PASSWORD=your-database-password
   JWT_SECRET=your-jwt-secret
   ```

2. **Using dotenv Package:** The dotenv package is used in development to load environment variables from the .env file into process.env. Make sure to add .env to your .gitignore to prevent it from being committed to version control.

   Install the dotenv package:

   bash

   ```
   npm install dotenv
   ```
   Load the .env file in your Node.js application:

   javascript

   ```
   require('dotenv').config();
   ```

```
const dbHost = process.env.DB_HOST;
const jwtSecret = process.env.JWT_SECRET;
```

b. Optimizing for Production

In production, performance is key. You should configure your API to handle requests efficiently and avoid unnecessary overhead.

1. **Set the NODE_ENV to Production:** This tells Node.js to run in production mode and enables various optimizations.

   Set the NODE_ENV environment variable in your production environment:

   bash

   ```
   export NODE_ENV=production
   ```

2. **Use a Reverse Proxy (e.g., Nginx):** In production, it's common to use a reverse proxy like Nginx to forward requests to your Node.js API. Nginx can handle tasks like load balancing, SSL termination, and serving static files.

3. **Enable Logging:** Use logging libraries like **Winston** or **Morgan** to log important events, errors, and HTTP requests for debugging and monitoring in production.

   Example using **Morgan** for HTTP logging:

   bash

```
npm install morgan
```

In your Node.js app:

```
javascript
```

```
const morgan = require('morgan');
app.use(morgan('combined'));
```

4. **Error Handling in Production:** Ensure that your error handling is set up properly. In production, you should display friendly error messages while logging the technical details to help you debug without exposing sensitive information to users.

---

2. Deploying to Cloud Platforms

Once your API is prepared, it's time to deploy it. There are several cloud platforms available that make it easy to deploy a Node.js application. Below are some common platforms for hosting Node.js APIs:

a. Deploying to Heroku

Heroku is one of the simplest platforms for deploying Node.js applications. It provides easy integration with Git, automatic scaling, and various add-ons for databases, caching, and more.

Steps to deploy to Heroku:

1. **Create a Heroku Account:** Sign up for a free Heroku account at https://www.heroku.com.

2. **Install the Heroku CLI:** Download and install the Heroku Command Line Interface (CLI) from https://devcenter.heroku.com/articles/heroku-cli.

3. **Deploy Your API:**
   - Initialize a Git repository in your project directory (if you haven't already):

     bash

     ```
     git init
     git add .
     git commit -m "Initial commit"
     ```

   - Log in to Heroku from the command line:

     bash

     ```
     heroku login
     ```

   - Create a Heroku app:

     bash

     ```
     heroku create
     ```

   - Push your code to Heroku:

bash

git push heroku master

- o Heroku will automatically detect your Node.js application and deploy it.
4. **Access Your API:** After deployment, Heroku provides a URL to access your API, typically in the form of https://your-app-name.herokuapp.com.

b. Deploying to AWS (Amazon Web Services)

For more control and scalability, you can deploy your Node.js API to AWS, using services like **EC2** (Elastic Compute Cloud) or **Elastic Beanstalk**.

Steps to deploy with **AWS Elastic Beanstalk**:

1. **Create an AWS Account:** Sign up for an AWS account at https://aws.amazon.com.
2. **Install the AWS Elastic Beanstalk CLI:** Download and install the Elastic Beanstalk CLI from https://docs.aws.amazon.com/elasticbeanstalk/latest/dg/eb-cli3-install.html.
3. **Initialize Elastic Beanstalk Environment:**
   - o From your project directory, initialize the Elastic Beanstalk environment:

bash

```
eb init
```

- o Follow the prompts to configure the application and set the region for deployment.

4. **Deploy to Elastic Beanstalk:**
   - o Create an Elastic Beanstalk environment:

   bash

   ```
   eb create
   ```

   - o Deploy your application:

   bash

   ```
   eb deploy
   ```

5. **Access Your API:** After deployment, Elastic Beanstalk provides a public URL for accessing your API.

---

3. Setting Up Continuous Integration/Continuous Deployment (CI/CD) Pipelines

Continuous Integration (CI) and **Continuous Deployment (CD)** are practices that allow you to automatically build, test, and deploy your application every time you make changes to your codebase.

Setting up a CI/CD pipeline streamlines the deployment process and reduces the chances of errors.

a. CI/CD Tools for Node.js APIs

- **GitHub Actions**: Automates workflows for testing and deploying your Node.js application.
- **CircleCI**: Provides integration with popular cloud platforms like AWS and Heroku.
- **Travis CI**: A hosted service that can automatically deploy your code to platforms like Heroku, AWS, or Google Cloud.

b. Example of a Simple CI/CD Pipeline with GitHub Actions

1. **Create a .github/workflows/deploy.yml file in your repository:** This file defines the workflow for deploying your Node.js API.

yaml

```
name: Deploy Node.js API to Heroku

on:
  push:
    branches:
      - main

jobs:
```

```
deploy:
  runs-on: ubuntu-latest
  steps:
    - name: Checkout code
      uses: actions/checkout@v2
    - name: Set up Node.js
      uses: actions/setup-node@v2
      with:
        node-version: '14'
    - name: Install dependencies
      run: npm install
    - name: Deploy to Heroku
      run: |
        git              remote              add              heroku
https://git.heroku.com/$HEROKU_APP_NAME.git
        git push heroku main
      env:
        HEROKU_API_KEY: ${{ secrets.HEROKU_API_KEY }}
```

2. **Set up your Heroku API Key as a secret:**

   o   Go to the **Settings** tab of your GitHub repository.

   o   Add your Heroku API Key as a secret under **Secrets** > **New repository secret**.

3. **Push Changes:** Once you push changes to the main branch, GitHub Actions will automatically trigger the deployment pipeline to Heroku.

With the steps outlined above, you now have a comprehensive understanding of how to prepare, deploy, and maintain your Node.js API in production. From cloud platforms like Heroku and AWS to setting up automated CI/CD pipelines, you can now deploy your API with confidence, knowing it's optimized for scalability, security, and ease of management.

By adopting best practices for deployment and integrating CI/CD, you ensure that your Node.js API is always up-to-date and reliable, providing seamless access to users and clients.